101 WAYS TO RUN THE OPTION

by Tony DeMeo

COACHES CHOICE™

ISBN: 1-57167-3687
Library of Congress Catalog Card Number: 98-89621

Diagrams: Janet Wahlfeldt
Cover Design: Matthew Edwards
Front Cover Photos: Courtesy of Washburn University
Back Cover Photos: Courtesy of The Topeka Capital-Journal
Developmental Editor: David Hamburg
Production Manager: Michelle A. Summers

Coaches Choice Books is a division of: Sagamore Publishing, Inc.
                                             P.O. Box 647
                                             Champaign, IL 61824-0647
                                             Web Site: http//www.sagamorepub.com

DEDICATION

This book is dedicated to my wife, Joanne, and my daughters Sara, Annie, Mary Kate and Michelle, who provide me with inspiration.

—T.D.

ACKNOWLEDGMENTS

This book would not have been possible without the help of the many coaches who have shared their ideas and been generous with their time. Some of these coaches have been mentioned in this book, but countless others have also either directly or indirectly contributed to the ideas presented here.

Finally, one last reminder: Football is one of the last institutions in this country that teaches and reinforces the values that have helped make this country the greatest on the planet. The values of character, courage, honor, and integrity will endure long after the score has been forgotten. Never forget that, as a coach, you are one of the guardians of those values that are under constant attack by those who disrespect both the law and our youth. As a wise man once said, *"In matters of truth and justice, never be afraid to stand alone."*

CONTENTS

Offensive football is a continuous evolution of principles and ideas. One of those ideas that has worked especially well for more than half a century is the option attack. The main reason the option offense has thrived throughout the years—and been improved on and modified—is that it embodies the always-sound principle of *two-on-one*.

This book was designed to stimulate the thinking of football coaches and give them a sampling of ideas regarding the option. Some sound advice for coaches who are interested in the details presented in this book is to research the topic: visit spring practices, watch videos, read books, and soak up as much knowledge as possible. It is that knowledge, along with an attention to details, that makes the difference in coaching. With the option, as with any type of offense, it is better to run three plays well than 10 plays poorly. Therefore, coaches should learn as much as they can about the option they want to use. Most coaches are willing to share ideas, so it is a good idea to call them and learn from them.

Another nugget of common sense is that a team should always maintain balance in its attack—not numerical balance, but rather a balance of capability. For instance, a team that is capable of running against a pass defense and passing against a run defense is a team that is balanced. Another example of a balanced team is one that runs power against a finesse defense and finesse against a power defense. The ability to be strategically flexible is a valuable asset to any football team. To paraphrase the Chinese philosopher Sun Tsu, *Your attack should have the form of water so it can adapt easily.* One-dimensional attacks will falter against teams of equal or superior talent, while flexible, multiple offenses will have a good chance to exploit a weakness in the defense and be effective.

HOW TO USE THIS BOOK

This book is filled with 101 option plays that coaches can incorporate into their offensive package—plays that they can install either in combination or as single plays.* It is recommended that coaches use this book as a sort of option menu from which they can make any number of selections. It is not recommended, however, that coaches try to run all the options described in the book.

As an aid to coaches, the book is divided into sections according to the various types of option systems available (see the Contents). Coaches should keep in mind, however, that the option plays provided in this book can be mixed and matched anyway they choose. As always, coaches are limited in their play selection only by the scope of their imagination and their ability to teach their players.

*In the diagrams of these option plays, the defender who is the handoff key has a square drawn around him; he is the give or keep key. The defender who represents the pitch key has a circle drawn around him; he is the pitch or keep key.

CHAPTER 1

Back to the Future

In football, as in life in general, the pendulum swings to and fro. Years ago, for example, the option play was popular with many college coaches. It carried Bud Wilkinson's University of Oklahoma teams to 47 consecutive victories and propelled Darrell Royal's University of Texas squads to two national titles. The option also helped catapult coaches such as Paul "Bear" Bryant, Tom Osborne, and Barry Switzer into national prominence, as their teams became the best in the country.

In recent years, however, college football has become saturated with high-powered passing attacks. Predictably, defenses have countered with in-your-face, man-to-man blitz packages as an antidote. However, by depending to a large degree on the blitz, modern defenses have left themselves vulnerable to their old nemesis, the option attack. To the chagrin of many defensive players and coaches, a number of offensive coaches have infused their passing attacks with various option plays.

As a result of its effectiveness, once again, the option play is being embraced by many of today's coaches as a staple of their offensive game plans. Clearly, the option is back in vogue.

Why the Option?

Coaches who are considering using the option as part of their offensive package will be interested in the following advantages it offers:

- It puts "speed in space" and therefore helps fast runners score points.

- It reduces the need for a dominant offensive line (i.e., since the quarterback's reads eliminate defenders, there are fewer defenders to block).

- It enables a physically inferior team to control the ball by running it, thus giving its defense more time to rest on the sideline.

- It forces the defense to play assignment football.

- It reduces the number of coverages that the defense can use.

- It forces the defense to run with "cover guys."

- It hampers the ability of the defense to blitz the quarterback, because he will be mobile and not stationary.

- It is easily adaptable to any formation.

- It is easily adaptable to any style of offense (e.g., run-and-shoot, I, wing T).

- It means that the option quarterback can be an athlete who is skilled at other positions. (This versatility is an advantage in an era of limited scholarships.)

- It enables the coach to have to train only one player to read a defense, rather than his entire offense.

- It is a goal-line-to-goal-line attack that requires no special red-zone or goal-line plays.

- It is also a sideline-to-sideline attack. As such, it stretches the defense horizontally and thus enables the offense to stretch and pierce as well.

- It is adaptable to multiple variations of motion.

- It enhances the passing game, because it forces the secondary to get involved with the run; therefore, it makes for a more complete offense.

- It enables the coach to have his game plan set from week to week, thus leaving him more time to tend to details and fine-tune his offense.

- It is a great overtime attack.

- It opens the door to more big plays, because it spreads the defense (e.g., the play-action pass can create big plays).

- It uses a variety of perimeter blocking schemes, thus simplifying the task of making game adjustments.

- It is adaptable to the team's personnel (e.g., if the team does not have a great running back, it can simply spread the ball around).

Rules for Installing the Option

Once a coach has decided to incorporate the option into his offensive game plan, he should consider the following criteria before he installs it:

- Commit to doing what you do well.

  —It's better to run a bad play well than a great play poorly.

- Keep the mesh point constant.

  —Although you can run multiple options, the effectiveness of your quarterback will be greater if your fullback is either directly behind the quarterback or over the guard, but not both (Diagram 1).

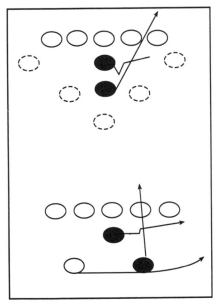

Diagram 1

- Devote an option period each day to practice all phases of your option attack.

- Take indecision out of your quarterback's reads by using "unless rules" (e.g., your quarterback says, "I am going to give off every time, *unless* the handoff key comes down flat and hard on the fullback").

  —Your quarterback is better off making a wrong read than a long read.

  —Teach your quarterback the proper thought process to use, and program that thought process with repetition.

- Your quarterback should always pitch the ball heart to heart (i.e., from his heart to the pitch man's heart).

- Adapt your blocking so that you are able to feature the ball carrier whom you want to carry the ball.

- Keep in mind that when you continue to put speed in space, big plays are bound to occur.

- Have a complementary play-action pass attack ready to exploit your opponent's secondary support.

- Have a complementary counter attack ready to exploit the defensive pursuit.

- Teach in terms of concepts and principles.

  —Your quarterback should be a student of the game.

- Never second-guess your quarterback's decision making, as long as he is following the proper thought process.

The Origins

The modern option game probably originated in the 1940s with Don Farout, who installed the split T in his University of Missouri offense. Bud Wilkinson subsequently embraced this attack at Oklahoma, and his Sooners promptly reeled off 47 consecutive victories. The key ingredient of the successful Sooner attack proved to be the large line splits that the split-T dictated. It was at Oklahoma that the concept of speed in space was born (Diagram 2).

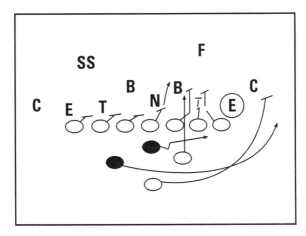

Diagram 2

The next big development in the option was the split-back veer attack introduced by Bill Yeomen at the University of Houston and Homer Rice at the University of Cincinnati. The veer signified the birth of the triple option and its revolutionary concept of adding a "read" to the option. It also transformed Houston and Cincinnati into big-play powerhouses. Rice also went a step further by including the drop-back pass in his option attack in order to put additional stress on opposing defenses.

At Texas and Texas A & M (respectively), a few years later, Darrell Royal and Emory Bellard further embellished the option by installing the wishbone, which was closer to the original split-T than to the veer: a three-back, ball-control attack that featured the running game. The main play in the wishbone, however, was the triple option.

Before long, other coaches were adapting the triple option to their attack. Most notable were Ken Hatfield and Fisher DeBerry at the Air Force Academy and Bob Sutton and Greg Gregory at Army, each of whom added his personal touch to the wishbone concept.

In recent years, many coaches have offered their own personalized take on the option attack:

- Gerry DiNardo employed the I-Bone to help lead Colorado to a national title and later used this offensive scheme to bring Vanderbilt to respectability.

- George DeLeone and Paul Pasqualoni at Syracuse University have helped to popularize the freeze and trap options; in the process, the Orangemen have gained national prominence as a gridiron power.

- At the University of Delaware, Tubby Raymond, along with his assistants Ted Kempski and Greg Perry, has utilized the triple option to spice up their vaunted Delaware Wing-T attack.

- University of Nebraska head coaches Tom Osborne and his successor, Frank Solich, have employed a complete option attack that has enabled the Cornhuskers to feast on their Big 12 opponents throughout the '90s.

It is interesting to note that success with the option attack has not been limited to major colleges. Pittsburg State (KS), for example, has done a great job of running the split-back veer and has one of the best records in Division II. In addition, Georgia Southern combined the run-and-shoot with the triple option to dominate Division IAA in the '80s.

CHAPTER 2

The Split-Back Veer

The forerunner of the modern option attack is the split-back veer offense, which was popularized by the University of Houston in the 1960s.*

*Coaches who are interested in researching and knowing more about the split-back veer will find it informative to talk with Chuck Broyles and his staff at Pittsburgh State University in Kansas. Coaches might also want to read Homer Rice's book, *Homer Rice on Triple Option Football.*

Advantages of the Split-Back Veer
- It puts three receivers on the line of scrimmage, which facilitates a pro-style passing game.

- Either of the two running backs can serve as the pitch man or the diveback.

- Large splits in the offensive line create space in the defensive front for the dive phase of the triple option.

- Using split backs allows both backs to release in pass patterns.

Disadvantages of the Split-Back Veer
- Since both backs are called on to run inside and outside, it is necessary that both of them possess similar skills.

- The position of the divebacks puts the quarterback-diveback mesh dangerously close to the handoff key, making it easier for the handoff key to disrupt the mesh and cause a fumble.

- The formation always has a strong side and a weak side, depending on the placement of the flanker.

OPTION#1: INSIDE VEER

The split-back inside veer is the basis of the triple-option offense. The quarterback is responsible for reading the handoff key (the first man outside the diveback's path) and optioning the pitch key (Diagram 3). The offensive line veer blocks and creates a running lane for the dive.

Assignments:
- Onside Guard—blocks the first downline man onside or inside.

- Onside Tackle—blocks the first linebacker onside or inside; if the guard is covered, uses a combo block.

- Center—blocks man onside, or linebacker onside or play side.

- Offside Guard and Tackle—cut off.

- Receivers—control the secondary defenders.

- Onside Wide Receiver—stalks onside corner.

- Offside Wide Receiver—cuts off.

- Tight End—stalks strong safety.

- Backs—take either the dive or the pitch.

- Onside Halfback—dives to the butt of the onside guard and reads his block if given the ball.

- Offside Halfback—takes pitch course.

The quarterback is the trigger. He reads the handoff key and gives off every time, *unless* the handoff key takes the dive. If the handoff key takes the dive, the quarterback comes down the line and options the pitch key. He pitches the ball to the offside halfback every time, *unless* the pitch key gets upfield or plays pitch. If the pitch key takes the pitch, the quarterback runs for a touchdown.

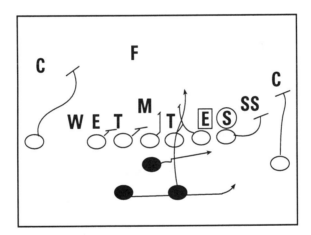

Diagram 3

OPTION # 2: OUTSIDE VEER

The first complement to the inside veer is the outside veer, which is the same triple option, only one hole wider. The quarterback is responsible for executing the same triple-option reads he did with the inside veer (Diagram 4). The offensive line creates a running lane for the dive.

Assignments:
- Onside Guard—blocks man onside or over.

- Onside Tackle—blocks first down lineman onside or inside. If uncovered, combo blocks with guard.

- Tight End—if tackle is covered, combos to first linebacker inside; if tackle is uncovered, releases directly to linebacker inside or to outside defensive end.

- Center and Offside Line—cut off.

- Wide Receivers—control secondary defenders (same as on inside veer).

- Onside Halfback—dives to the butt of onside tackle and executes triple option.

- Offside Halfback—takes pitch course.

- Quarterback—executes triple-option reads one man wider; gives unless pitch key plays the pitch.

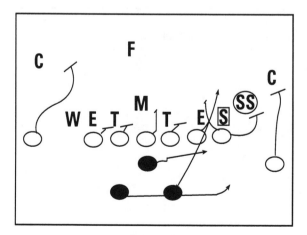

Diagram 4

OPTION #3: LEAD OPTION

The next option in the split-back veer attack is the lead option, which is a double option (pitch or keep). The Lead Option is a good way to get the ball on the perimeter (Diagram 5).

Assignments:
- The offensive line and the tight end execute wide veer rules, unless the onside tackle is uncovered. If the onside tackle is uncovered, the tackle blocks the linebacker over him to the middle backer. The tight end takes an outside release, blocking the outside linebacker over the tackle, if the outside linebacker escapes the offensive tackle's block. If the tackle blocks the outside linebacker, the tight end can go up to the safety (Diagram 6).

- The onside halfback arc blocks the strong safety.

- The offside halfback is the pitch man.

- The quarterback takes a drop step and options the end man on the line, using his normal pitch/keep decision-making process.

- The wide receivers stalk and cut off the secondary defenders, just as they do on all options.

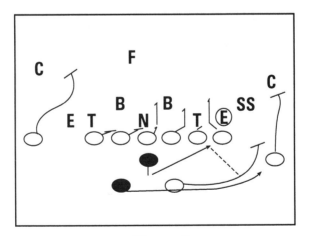

Diagram 5

OPTION #4: COUNTER LEAD OPTION

The counter lead option is the same as the lead option, except that the entire backfield reverses out before executing their assignments (Diagram 6). This counter action freezes the inside linebackers, making it easier for the tight end to seal them.

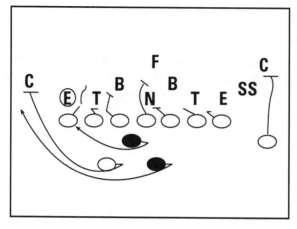

Diagram 6

OPTION #5: LOAD OPTION

The Load Option is an excellent complement to the lead option. This play was run to perfection by Texas Christian University, under Coach Jim Wacker. It is a double option that is used to get the ball on the perimeter. It is a particularly effective option for those teams that have a talented running quarterback (Diagram 7).

The assignments are exactly the same as they are on the lead option, except that the onside halfback load blocks either the defensive end or the end man on the line, instead of arc blocking the strong safety. The quarterback takes the ball to the strong safety and executes the options off of him rather than the defensive end.

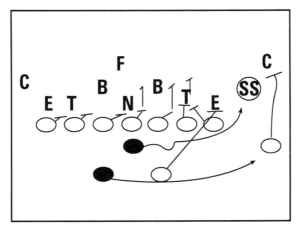

Diagram 7

OPTION #6: COUNTER DIVE OPTION

The Counter Dive Option is an excellent misdirection double option that can be particularly effective if it is properly set up by the counter dive. The key block is made by the onside tackle, who must reach the man over him. The onside tackle's block is made easier if the dive has been established before the option is run (Diagram 8).

Assignments:

- Offensive Line—base blocks man over.

- Tight End—arcs on the strong safety.

- Onside Halfback—dives to the onside cheek of the center and fakes the counter dive.

- Offside Halfback—reverses out and gets on his pitch course.

- Quarterback—reverse pivots and fakes the counter dive; then executes the option on the defensive end.

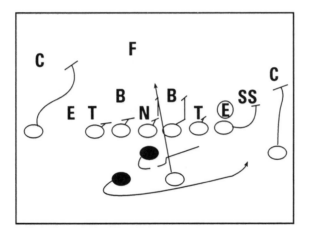

Diagram 8

OPTION #7: PITT STATE OPTION

By adding a pulling guard to the counter lead option, the Pittsburgh State staff made it even more potentially devastating. In the Pitt State Option, the onside offensive line veer blocks, just as it does on the triple option. However, the center must post and set to cut off for the pulling guard. The offside pulls flat down the line of scrimmage and blocks the onside linebacker. The offside tackle seals and wheels backside. The backfield executes the counter lead option. The tight end is flexed and cracks the linebacker to the safety (Diagram 9). On the other side, the split end stalks the corner, and the onside halfback blocks the outside linebacker (Diagram 10). The Pitt State options are almost a complete offense in themselves and are excellent additions to the split-back veer.

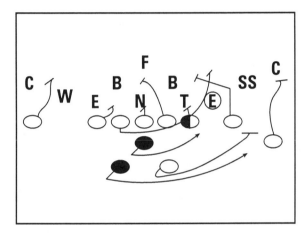

Diagram 9

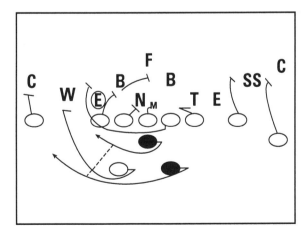

Diagram 10

OPTION #8: WIDENER OPTION

This option is known as the Widener Option, a devastating double option run by Bill Manlove and his staff during the late 1970s and early 1980s, when Widener University (PA) was dominating Division III football. This play works especially well if the guard is capable of blocking the strong safety (Diagram 11).

The onside offensive tackle and slotback use the same lead option rules that the tackle and tight end use. If the tackle is covered, they combo up to the linebacker. The key block on this play is by the onside guard, who pulls and then blocks the strong safety. The offside line uses its cutoff rules.

The backfield executes its triple-option technique, except that the quarterback fakes to the diveback and then executes the option off the defensive end. The coaching point for the diveback is that he must be prepared to pick up the onside linebacker.

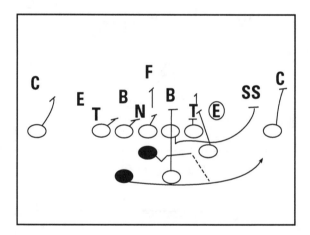

Diagram 11

OPTION #9: CRAZY OPTION

The Crazy Option is another counter option that is intended to slow down pursuit and get the ball pitched on the perimeter. Lou Holtz and his staff developed this option while Holtz was the head coach was at the University of Arkansas (Diagram 12). The Crazy Option is an excellent double option. Not only is it a good companion play for the trap, but it is also an effective key breaker.

The offensive line blocks using trap option rules. The onside line veer blocks. The center posts the man on him and turns and seals backside. The backside guard has the key block; he pulls and logs the first man outside the tackle's block. The guard's block can be set up by running the trap play to the diveback. The backside tackle seals and wheels.

The backfield action is a little different. The offside halfback fakes the counter dive and fills for the pulling guard. The onside halfback whirly steps and becomes the pitch man. The quarterback does a 360-degree pivot, faking the counter dive, and then comes down the line of scrimmage to option the end man on the line. The quarterback must be alert to quick pressure from the defensive end.

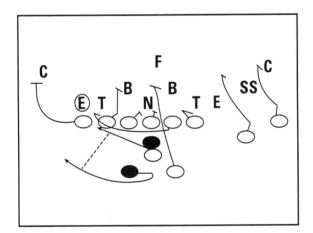

Diagram 12

OPTION #10: HARD OPTION

Some split-back veer teams run a triple option in which they block the handoff key (thus the name "Hard Option") in order to make the read easier for the quarterback (see Diagram 13). In the Hard Option, the quarterback simply reads "daylight." If the handoff key widens and the quarterback sees daylight for the diveback to run through, the quarterback gives the ball; but if the handoff key closes down and there is no daylight, the quarterback pulls and options the defensive end.

This option is a low-risk option, because a blocked handoff key cannot crash on the mesh and thereby cause a fumble. The only problem with this option is that it is only good against certain defenses; it must be packaged, therefore it is limited in its use.

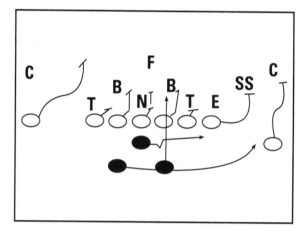

Diagram 13

CHAPTER 3

THE WISHBONE

The time- and battle-tested Wishbone Offense has been the most productive rushing offense in the history of the college game.* Developed by Darrell Royal and his staff at the University of Texas, the wishbone took the Longhorns to two national championships and a 30-game winning streak. Barry Switzer's Oklahoma teams set numerous records while running a high-octane version of the original wishbone, and Ken Hatfield, Pepper Rodgers, Fisher DeBerry, and even the legendary Bear Bryant have all put their imprint on this potent three-back attack.

*Coaches interested in exploring the wishbone in depth should read *Installing the Wishbone T* by Pepper Rodgers and Homer Smith. They can also talk with either Ken Hatfield at Rice University or Fisher DeBerry and Bob Noblit at the Air Force Academy.

The Advantages of the Wishbone

- It is completely balanced—the option can be run to either side with a lead blocker.

- It depends on specialized backs—the fullback is strictly an inside runner and the halfbacks are strictly outside runners.

- Large offensive line splits create natural holes for the fullback dives.

- The mesh point is removed from the handoff key, making the read less likely to result in a fumble.

- Because only the fullback runs the mesh, it can be mastered more easily than it would if the two halfbacks were possible divebacks.

- The relationship between the pitch man and the lead blocker is more effective than the relationship between the tight end and the halfback in the split-back veer.

- A three-back attack is more conducive to the implementation of a power game.

- The wishbone is an unselfish, team-oriented attack.

The Disadvantages of the Wishbone

- Having only two receivers on the line of scrimmage limits the passing game.

- Using three running backs could be problematic on a team with little depth in that department.

- The wishbone halfbacks must be blockers as well as runners; they must be big enough to block and fast enough to be pitch men.

- Because the wishbone is predominantly a run-oriented offense, a team that features it will have difficulty recruiting talented wide receivers and accurate passing quarterbacks.

- The wishbone is not a productive two-minute attack or come-from-behind offense.

OPTION #11: LOOP TRIPLE OPTION TO THE SPLIT END

The triple option is the base play of the wishbone attack, just as it was in the split-back veer offense. However, the triple option from the wishbone can be run with "loop blocking," because in this case, the mesh is further removed from the handoff key (Diagram 14).

Assignments:
The offensive linemen step with their play-side foot and take an outside release to their assignments.

- Onside Tackle—loop releases outside the handoff key to the play-side linebacker.

- Onside Guard—the first man onside or outside, on or off the line.

- Center—loops to offside linebacker.

- Offside Guard—reaches the man on the center or the cutoff man onside.

- Offside Tackle—cuts off.

- Split End—stalks man on.

- Onside Halfback— arc forces defender.

- Offside Halfback—pitch man.

- Fullback—runs triple course to butt of onside guard.

- Quarterback—executes triple-option reads.

The Loop Triple Option to the Split End is one of the best split end attacks in football. The loop scheme was basically designed to defeat the 50 defense and the pinch-and-scrape stunt by the defensive tackle and the linebacker. The complementary option is the same scheme to the tight end.

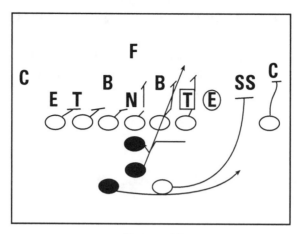

Diagram 14

OPTION #12: LOOP TRIPLE OPTION TO THE TIGHT END

When defenses start overplaying the split end flank by inverting their strong safety up and filling with their free safety, the loop to the tight end comes in handy and serves as the offense's counter (Diagram 15). In this option, the offensive line blocks exactly as it does on the loop to the split end side. The backfield play is also the same. The only difference is that the tight end takes an outside release and blocks the free safety.

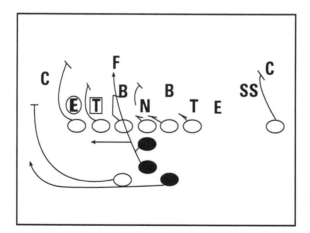

Diagram 15

OPTION #13: WISHBONE COUNTER DIVE OPTION

A great misdirection option is the Wishbone Counter Dive Option that was popularized in the '70s by Pepper Rodgers at UCLA. This option is a direct descendant of the split-back veer counter dive option, except that it uses the fullback as the lead blocker (Diagram 16).

Assignments:

- Offensive Line—reach blocks man over.

- Tight End—blocks the free safety after taking an outside release.

- Onside Halfback—jab steps up at a 45-degree angle and dives to the near cheek of the guard and fakes the counter dive.

- Fullback—jabs away and arc blocks the force defender.

- Offside Halfback—jabs away and becomes the pitch man.

- Quarterback—reverse pivots, fakes the counter dive, and then executes the option on the defensive end.

The key block is made by the onside tackle on the defensive tackle. This block must be set up by running the counter dive prior to the option. If the onside tackle is having problems reaching the defensive tackle, the counter dive should be successful because it will hit inside the defensive tackle.

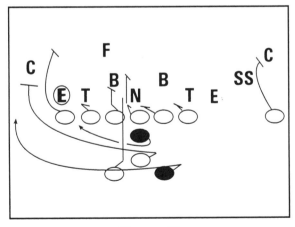

Diagram 16

OPTION #14: VEER OPTION

The Veer Option is an effective complement to the tight-end attack. If the defensive front is mirroring the offensive line, the offense can run the loop scheme to get a give read and then the veer scheme to get the defensive line to squeeze down and to get a pull read and probably a pitch (Diagram 17). On this play, the backfield executes the triple option the same way it has on the previous triple options.

Assignments:

The offensive line veer blocks or down blocks. The linemen step with their inside foot and release inside to their assignments, just as they did on the split-back triple option. The key blocks are made by the guard and the tackle. The guard blocks the first-down-line man, and the tackle "veer releases" to the play-side linebacker. If the guard is covered, then the tackle combos up to the linebacker.

The unique block on the Veer Option is made by the tight end, who also veer releases if the tackle is covered and then blocks the play-side linebacker to the free safety. If the defensive end closes with the tight end, the pitch should probably be made. This scheme offers a wonderful opportunity to veer block against a 50 defense and handle the pinch-and-scrape stunt by the defensive tackle and the linebacker.

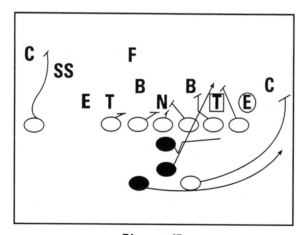

Diagram 17

OPTION #15: VEER OPTION TO UNBALANCED

Those coaches who want to use the same scheme as the veer option to get the ball pitched to the wide side of the field should simply take the tight end and put him to the same side as the split end to form an unbalanced formation. The Veer Option to Unbalanced is executed exactly as the previous option (#14), except that the split end can crack the force defender and the halfback can arc the corner playing over the split end (Diagram 18).

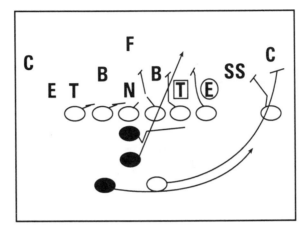

Diagram 18

OPTION #16: TOAD OPTION

One defensive adjustment that teams use to make it difficult for the lead halfback to block the corner is to bring the corner tight to the line of scrimmage to the tight end side. The offense can counter, however, by employing the Toad Option, which is one of the most effective goal-line triple options available. In the Toad Option, the offense makes an adjustment in its wishbone by having the tight end "toad block" the defensive end (who is the normal pitch key) and make the corner the pitch key instead. The rest of the team executes the veer option, except that the onside halfback seal blocks the onside linebacker. The halfback, meanwhile, reads the tackle/tight end up and blocks to the linebacker inside or outside the tight end's block (Diagram 19).

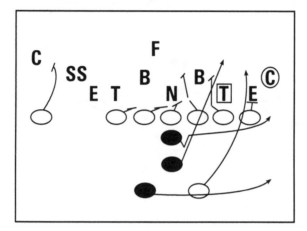

Diagram 19

OPTION#17: SEAL OPTION

The birth of the reduced defense, or the eight-man front, led to the development of the Seal Option to the Split End (Diagram 20) as a counter.

Assignments:
The offensive line veer blocks, placing emphasis on movement at the point of attack. The offensive backfield executes its triple-option assignments. The major difference between the seal and the toad is that, although in the seal, the onside halfback seals the play-side linebacker the way he does in the Toad Option, he doesn't have a tight end's block to read. In the meantime, the quarterback reads the defensive end and options the strong safety.

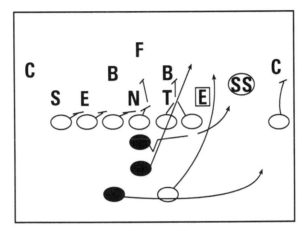

Diagram 20

OPTION #18: LOAD OPTION

The Load Option is another good short-yardage, tight end option that is a direct descendant of the split back veer offense. It complements the veer option to the tight end and also serves as an adjustment to a hard corner to the tight end side (Diagram 21). It is an especially effective option for those teams with a great running quarterback.*

The offensive line and backfield execute the veer option (see Option #14), except that the onside halfback "load blocks" the defensive end by putting his shoulder through the defensive end's outside thigh. The quarterback, who normally reads the defensive tackle, instead options the corner as he does in the toad option (see Option #16). What essentially is happening in the Load Option is that the tight end and the halfback are exchanging their assignments from the toad option.

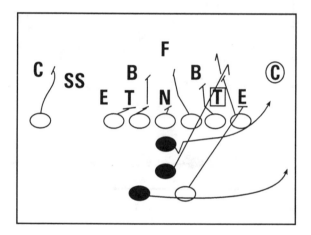

Diagram 21

*Harry Gamble's teams at the University of Pennsylvania set all of the school's rushing records while using this option.

OPTION #19: G OPTION TO THE SPLIT END

Another effective tactic that can be employed against the reduced defense is the "G" block: The G blocking scheme* has the offensive tackle block down on the man over the guard, while the guard folds around the tackle's block to block the linebacker.

The key coaching point for the guard is as follows: If the handoff squeezes the offensive tackle down, the guard can go *around* the handoff key to the linebacker; but if the handoff key stays wide on upfield, the guard can go *inside* the handoff key for the linebacker. Against a reduced defense, the guard will probably go inside the handoff key; against a 50 defense, he will probably go around. For its part, the backfield executes the seal triple option (Diagram 22).

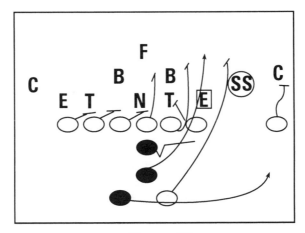

Diagram 22

*The G options add variety to the wishbone by changing the interior blocking schemes so that the guard folds around the offensive tackle's block in order to block the linebacker. Former Northeastern offensive coordinator John Strollo ran this scheme in the 1980s, enabling his teams to set several school rushing records.

OPTION #20: G OPTION TO THE TIGHT END

This option complements the G option to the split end side by offering subtle differences (Diagram 23). As in Option #19, the offensive line G blocks; however, the tight end toad blocks the end man on the line of scrimmage, and the onside halfback seals the linebacker to the safety *outside* the tight end's block. The backfield executes the triple option, and the quarterback should expect to be running. Those teams blessed with a speedster at quarterback should take advantage of this scheme.

The great advantage of the G block to the tight end side is that the offense can neutralize the filling free safety by blocking him with the lead halfback. Of course, the key is to have guards athletic enough to block linebackers.

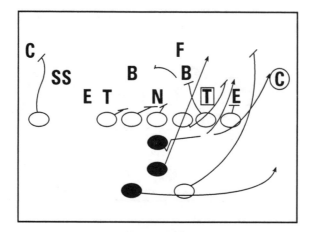

Diagram 23

The Rock Options

The Rock Options are two double options designed to get the ball pitched. Teams that have either a quarterback with limited running ability or a halfback they definitely want to feature may find success with the rock option, which was popularized by Greg Gregory at Army in the 1980s. The rock option is an offshoot of the split-back veer counter lead option and is especially conducive to the pitch.

OPTION #21: ROCK OPTION TO THE TIGHT END*

In the Rock Option to the Tight End, the offensive line has exactly the same assignments it has in the wide veer in the split-back veer (see Option #2). By releasing the tight end inside, the offense influences the defensive end to close, thus providing a pitch read.

The offensive backfield jab steps in the opposite direction and then executes its assignments. The lead halfback arc blocks the corner, while the fullback goes around the pitch key and seals the onside linebacker. The offside halfback jabs and then becomes the pitch man. The quarterback takes his triple-step away and then turns into the line of scrimmage and options the defensive end (Diagram 24).

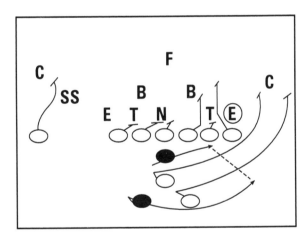

Diagram 24

*This option is one of two "Rock" options designed to get the ball pitched. Popularized by Army's Greg Gregory in the '80s, the rock options are designed to help a team that has a quarterback who is a limited threat as a runner, but has a halfback who can scamper. The rock options were born of the split-back veer counter lead option and enable the quarterback to pitch the ball very effectively.

OPTION #22: ROCK OPTION TO THE SPLIT END

The Rock Option to the Split End side is a valuable weapon against the reduced defense (Diagram 25). In this scheme, the offensive line veer blocks to the split end side, and the backfield executes the same technique that it does to the tight end side. The key to this play is that it can only be run to a reduced front. Consequently, a coach would probably have to package this play with its tight end version (Option #21).

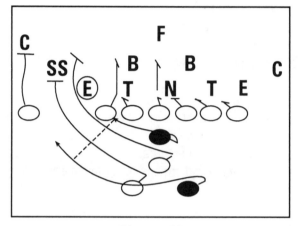

Diagram 25

OPTION #23: WIDE VEER

The Wide Veer, a play run by Emory Bellard at Texas A&M in the '70s, complements the inside veer nicely. In this variation of the wishbone, the offensive line has the same blocking assignments as in the split-back veer option (see Option #2). The basic coaching point, however, is that the line must cheat its splits to two feet, because the fullback has a tougher angle from which to get to the mesh point in the wishbone than the halfback has in the split-back veer.

The backfield assignments in the Wide Veer are the same as in the seal triple option, but with a few minor adjustments:

- The onside halfback seals outside the defensive end, who is the handoff key.

- The fullback's aiming point is the butt of the tackle.

- The quarterback, in order to get to the wider mesh point, must take either a pop-step or an elongated first step.

- The key to the success of this play is the movement by the tackle and tight end at the point of attack (Diagram #26).

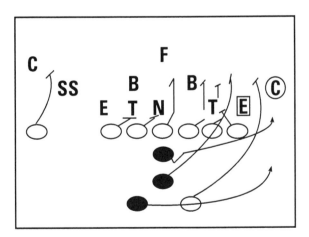

Diagram 26

OPTION #24: HALFBACK WIDE VEER

The Halfback Wide Veer is virtually a duplicate of the wide veer out of the split-back veer offense, with the offensive line's blocking assignments the same as in all wide veers (Diagram 27). The backfield action in this option is the same as in the split-back veer (Option #2), with the exception that the fullback seals the linebacker. In addition, the onside halfback dives to the butt of the tackle, and the quarterback comes down the line, reads the defensive end, and options the corner. It should be noted that some coaches may choose not to run this option as part of the wishbone package, because the mesh point is too markedly different from all the other mesh points in the wishbone.

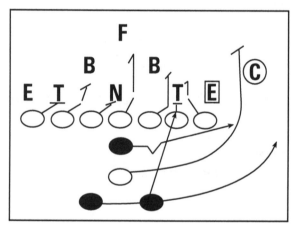

Diagram 27

OPTION #25: WISHBONE DOWN OPTION

Taken from the Delaware Wing-T, the Wishbone Down Option is intended to feature a good running quarterback and to be effective against a seven-man front. It is a double option that gets the quarterback on the perimeter to the tight end side. One of the great aspects of this option is that either the fullback or the lead halfback can block the free safety (Diagram 28). The two primary coaching points are first that the lead backs roll around the guard's block and do not let anyone cross their face and second that the offside halfback is the pitch man.

Assignments:
- Tight End—the tight end blocks down on the first defender on or off the line of scrimmage.

- Onside Tackle—blunts the man on him if the guard is uncovered, and then he blocks a fill linebacker to the nose guard; if the guard is covered, the tackle must come right down on the man who is on the guard.

- Center—protects play-side gap; blocks the man onside or squeezes the man who is over the play-side guard.

- Onside Guard—pulls flat and logs the end man on the line of scrimmage, as in a "guard load."

- Offside Line—uses its cutoff rules.

- Onside Halfback—seals the onside linebacker to the free safety.

- Fullback—reads the guard's block and goes inside or outside that block and seals the linebacker.

- Quarterback—reverse pivots and gets on the outside hip of the guard and reads his block.

  —If the guard logs the defensive end, the quarterback should get into the perimeter and option the corner.

  —If the guard cannot log the defensive end because the defensive end is either upfield or widening, the quarterback should duck inside the guard's block and follow the fullback.

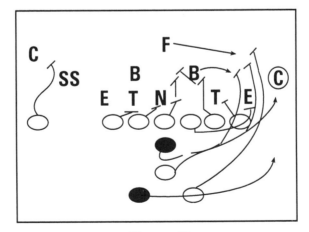

Diagram 28

OPTION #26: WISHBONE COUNTER TRAP OPTION

The Wishbone Counter Trap Option is a great misdirection option that helps slow down linebacker pursuit (Diagram 29). This double option is also an effective pitch option, and it gives the tight end the opportunity to block the free safety alley player. The only coaching point for this option is for the center, who should post his man onside before sealing the back side.

Assignments

- The onside offensive line veer blocks as usual.

- The offside guard pulls flat and logs the first man outside the tackle's block (the handoff key), while the offside tackle seals and wheels.

- The tight end can perform an inside or outside release (depending on how the defensive end is playing) and then block the linebacker to the free safety.

- The halfbacks jab-step away and execute their normal arc option. The lead blocker arcs the corner, and the offside halfback is the pitch man.

- The fullback fills the offside guard-center gap and looks for any backer who runs through.

- The quarterback triple-steps opposite, flash fakes to the fullback, and then turns back into the line of scrimmage and jumps into the guard's hip pocket. If the guard can log the defensive tackle, then the quarterback should option the defensive end. If the guard cannot log the defensive tackle, then the quarterback should duck up inside the guard's block (as in a quarterback trap).

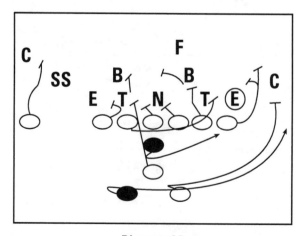

Diagram 29

OPTION #27: G DOUBLE OPTION

With many of today's defenses inclined to use the free-safety fill as a means to thwart the quarterback, offenses need to vary their blocking schemes. In the G Double Option, the G block is put on the linebacker, while the fullback blocks the free safety. The result of this blocking scheme is a very effective double option that should feature a star halfback (Diagram 30).

Assignments:
- The offensive line G blocks the same way it does on the G triple option (see Option #19).

- The onside halfback arc blocks the strong safety; the offside halfback is the pitch back.

- The fullback blocks the linebacker, if the linebacker escapes the guard's G block; but if the linebacker is blocked, then the fullback moves to the free safety.

- The quarterback executes the double option by flash faking to the fullback and then optioning the defensive end.

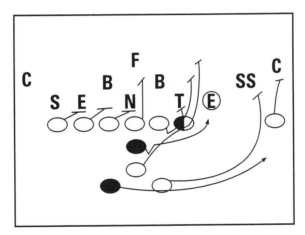

Diagram 30

OPTION #28: KEEP OPTION

The Keep Option is one of the simplest of all the double options. It is extremely effective against a defense that squeezes the offensive tackle's veer release. It is also a good option to run against a sit-and-read handoff key (Diagram #31). The offensive line simply veer blocks. The only coaching point for the linemen is that they can tighten their splits in order to shorten the flank.

Assignments:
- The backfield executes the seal option, except that the fullback blocks the handoff key by running his shoulder through the outside thigh of the handoff key.

- The quarterback flash fakes the fullback and then accelerates to option the strong safety.

One other coaching point should be noted: If the handoff key works outside, the halfback loads him and the fullback blocks the linebacker to the safety. The quarterback should then follow the fullback and duck inside the halfback's block.

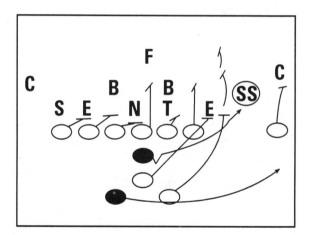

Diagram 31

CHAPTER 4

THE I-BONE

The I-Bone was introduced at the University of Colorado under the direction of Bill McCartney and his offensive coordinator, Gerry DiNardo. McCartney's Buffaloes won the national championship running the I-Bone. Soon after, DiNardo took the I-Bone to Vanderbilt University where he led the Commodores back to respectability in the Southeastern Conference. Obviously evolved directly from the wishbone, the I-Bone features the same blocking schemes and concepts.

Advantages of the I-Bone

- It employs specialized backs as follows:

  —The fullback is strictly an inside runner.

  —The upback is strictly a blocker and a counter runner.

  —The tailback is the pitch back and the featured runner.

- It is completely balanced to either side.

- It can feature one star tailback who runs both inside on power plays and outside on pitch plays to both sides.

Disadvantages of the I-Bone

- All the backs are stacked between the guards, making it easier for the defense to read.

- Having all the backs stacked makes it more difficult to seal the linebackers, because when facing the I-Bone, the linebackers are never outflanked by any of the backs.

- Having the backs stacked makes it more difficult to get the backs out in pass routes.

OPTION #29: I-BONE TOAD

The I-Bone Toad option calls for the same blocking assignments as the wishbone toad option (see Option #16). The only difference is the backfield alignment and the short motion by the upback to get into proper position to seal the linebacker (Diagram 32). This option is an excellent goal-line and short-yardage triple-option play.

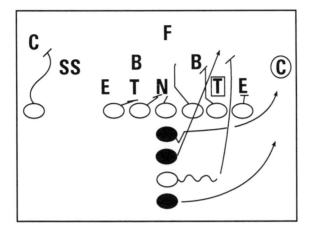

Diagram 32

OPTION #30: I-BONE DOUBLE OPTION

One of the basic principles espoused by LSU head coach Gerry DiNardo is that if a handoff key is easy to read, he is hard to block; and if he is hard to read, he is easy to block. This tenet explains why double options are a staple of the I-Bone attack.

For the offensive line, the assignments are exactly the same as in the wishbone rock option to the split end side—the line just veer blocks (see Option #22). The backfield action, however, is a little different. The upback goes into his slide motion and arcs the strong safety. The fullback runs his triple course and blocks from linebacker to free safety. The tailback is the pitch man. The quarterback flash fakes the fullback and pitches off the defensive end (Diagram 33). This play offers a wonderful opportunity for an offense to get its top runner on the perimeter and optimize speed in space.

This option works best against a reduced defense and can be G blocked, as in Option #27. It also provides an excellent opportunity for a team's top runner to get out on the perimeter for the ultimate in speed in space.

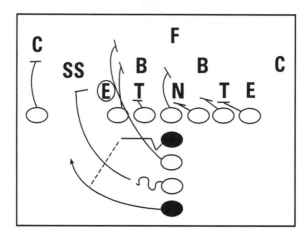

Diagram 33

CHAPTER 5

WOODY'S OPTIONS

Ohio State's Woody Hayes was the coach who was always associated with a "three yards and a cloud of dust" offense, but he was also very effective with the option. Although it is true that Hayes was a conservative play caller, he was clearly a brilliant tactician and strategist who put his own mark on the option game. His book *Hot-Line to Victory* is a football text that should be read by every coach.

Hayes favored two options: (1) the option he ran out of his standard I formation and (2) his Robust T goal-line option. Both of those options were effective because they were executed with the level of precision that helped make Woody Hayes a coaching legend.

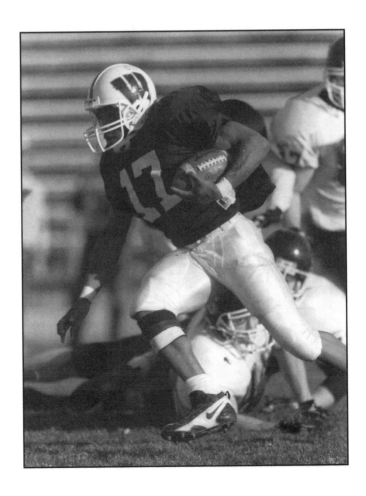

OPTION #31: ROBUST T OPTION

The Robust T Option was the hallmark of Woody Hayes's goal-line attack. It was a full-house, two-tight end, get-after-it offense. The Robust T was set up by the fullback off-tackle play, which happened to be the base play of this formation.

In the Robust T, the offensive line has the same blocking assignments as in the split-back load option (see Option #5). The line essentially base blocks, with the tight end and the tackle double-teaming if the tackle is covered.

Assignments:
- The onside halfback load blocks the end man on the line of scrimmage by driving his shoulder through the outside thigh of the defensive end.

- The fullback runs his belly course to the outside cheek of the tackle; he makes a good fake and then dents the line of scrimmage.

- The quarterback reverse pivots and gives a good fake to the fullback; he then progresses down the line of scrimmage to option the corner.

- The offside halfback is the pitch man (Diagram 34).

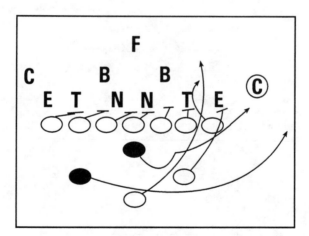

Diagram 34

OPTION #32: I-SLOT OPTION

The I-Slot Option was also effective for Hayes in short-yardage situations, and it is a close cousin of the Robust T.* It is a double option, but does not involve any inside fake to the fullback. Instead, it is a lead option that uses the fullback as a lead blocker (Diagram 35).

The offensive line blocks the same assignments as in the Robust T; the only difference is that the tight slot takes the place of the tight end and doubles with the onside tackle.

Assignments:
- The fullback arc blocks the strong safety.

- The tailback is the pitch man.

- The quarterback drop steps and then comes down the line and options the defensive end.

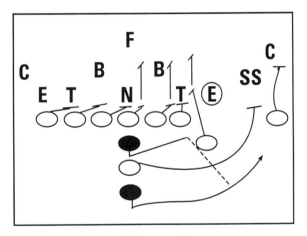

Diagram 35

*Although Ohio State doesn't run either the Robust T or the I-Slot options, another school currently in Ohio has had great success with them. Coaches who would like more details about these options should get in touch with Mike Kelly at the University of Dayton.

CHAPTER 6

THE DELAWARE WING-T

With regard to the Delaware Wing-T, when most coaches think of the modern masters of the game, and when all factors are considered, the names of Tubby Raymond and Ted Kempski come to mind. Tubby, Ted, and offensive line coach Greg Perry do an unbelievable job of coaching offensive football at the University of Delaware, home of the Fighting Blue Hens. In essence, the Delaware Wing-T is designed to mix the curveballs of the buck sweep/waggle series with fastball option plays.*

*It is recommended that coaches who wish to find out more about the Delaware Wing-T offensive scheme take advantage of Tubby Raymond's series of five books and five videos on the wing-T (available through Coaches Choice Books and Videos). Coaches may also want to take a trip to the University of Delaware to learn the nuances of the plays that are described in this section.

OPTION #33: DOWN OPTION

The Down Option is my personal favorite wing-T option, because it raises conflict for the defensive end and makes it easier for the fullback to slip around and block the free safety. On this play, the offensive line blocks down option rules (see Option #25: Wishbone Down Option). This assignment is basically a guard load (i.e., the guard blocks the end man on the line).

Assignments:

- The wingback seals the inside linebacker, thus exploiting the major advantage of the Delaware Wing-T, which is that the lead blocker is in a super position to seal block on all options. The position of the wingback outflanks the onside linebacker, making his block a simple one.

- The offside halfback uses a two-step motion and is the pitch man.

- The fullback runs his belly course to the outside leg of the tackle and fakes the down play on which he carries the ball. After the fake, the fullback should get on the pulling guard's outside hip and then wrap around so he can block the free safety.

- The quarterback reverse pivots, fakes the fullback belly, and gets on the hip of the guard and reads his block. If the guard logs the defensive end, the quarterback should get around the guard's block and option the comer. If the guard cannot log the defensive end, the quarterback should duck inside the guard's block and follow the fullback (Diagram 36).

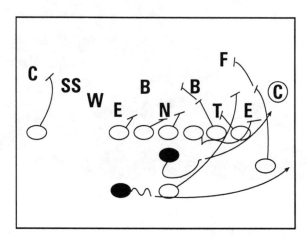

Diagram 36

OPTION #34: CROSS-BLOCK OPTION

The Cross-Block Option complements the split end side of the Delaware Wing-T Option game (Diagram 37). In it, the option is set up by running the cross-block belly play, which is a staple of the wing-T attack. It is an excellent way to get the ball on the perimeter and away from the wingback.

The offensive line blocks the same assignments as the Wishbone G double option, except that the guard logs the defensive end, making this scheme much like a guard load. The tackle comes down hard on the defensive tackle, and the rest of the line scoops play side. The coaching point for the center is that he must protect his play-side gap.

Assignments:
- The onside halfback seal blocks on the play-side linebacker, while the offside halfback goes in motion to become the pitch man.

- The fullback fakes the belly play and then tries to get downfield to block the free safety by wrapping around the guard's block.

- The quarterback reverses out, fakes the belly, accelerates around the guard's block, and options the strong safety.

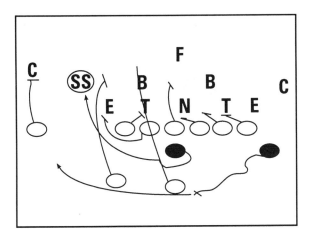

Diagram 37

OPTION #35: DELAWARE TRAP OPTION

The Delaware Wing-T Trap Option is a wonderful complement to the fullback trap: the buck sweep complements the trap to the wing side, and the trap option complements the trap to the slot side (Diagram 38).

The offensive line uses the same trap-option blocking used in the wishbone trap option (see Option #16). The backfield action is also the same as in the wishbone trap action, except that the quarterback reverse pivots, fakes the trap to the fullback, and then works down the line to option the defensive end.

The perimeter blocking is different, however, because the wing-T uses the trap option primarily as a split end play. The split end cracks the strong safety, and the slot back arcs on the corner. This blocking scheme sets up the trap-option pass.

In Tubby Raymond's view, every play is more effective if it is part of a sequence, because it is the sequence that creates conflicts in defensive reads. Clearly, the trap, the trap option, and the trap-option pass form an outstanding sequence that poses conflict for the defensive tackle, who must ask: "Do I close on the trap or play the trap option?"

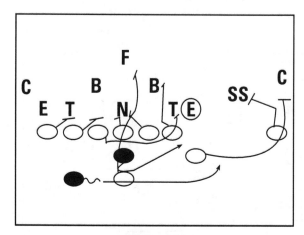

Diagram 38

OPTION #36: WING-T LEAD OPTION

In the wing-T, the fullback has become more of a tailback than a true fullback; thus it is a good idea to get the ball to him on the perimeter. The Wing-T Lead Option to the fullback allows such a maneuver, and it also enhances the effectiveness of the wing-T by giving it a good, simple option away from the slot (Diagram 39). In addition, the lead option is an effective complement to the trap option in the slot set.

The assignments for the lead option are exactly the same as they are in the split-back veer lead option (see Option #3). The only difference is that the lead halfback blocks the corner and the fullback is the pitch man.

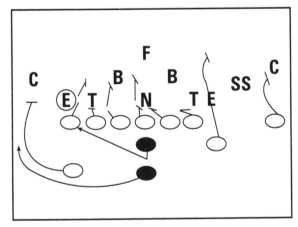

Diagram 39

OPTION #37: COUNTER CRISSCROSS

The Delaware Wing-T Counter Crisscross is not a true option; however, the halfback who is the ball carrier has the option to pitch the ball back to the quarterback (Diagram 40). This play perhaps underscores the diversity of the Delaware Wing-T and indicates precisely why—despite its complexity—the Delaware Wing-T is a complete package of offensive football. On this play, the onside offensive line counter blocks.

Assignments:
- Onside Tackle—down blocks to the first man on or off the line of scrimmage.

- Onside Guard—also blocks down.

- Center—posts and seals for the back-side guard.

- Offside Guard—pulls and blocks inside-out.

- Offside Tackle—seals and wheels.

- Tight End—pulls and leads through the hole.

- Fullback—dives for the tackle's butt and seals for the tight end.

- Quarterback—reverse pivots, gives the ball to the halfback, and then gets on the boot course.

- Right Halfback—receives the ball from the quarterback and then hands it on an inside handoff to the left halfback.

- Left Halfback—receives the ball from the right halfback and follows the tight end. If the hole is closed, he should look to pitch the ball to the quarterback.

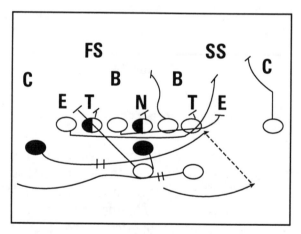

Diagram 40

CHAPTER 7

MULTIPLE I OPTIONS

Many coaches have added to the option game from the Pro I formation.* The Pro I formation puts three receivers on the line of scrimmage in order to enhance the passing game. This formation also calls for specialized backfield play. The fullback runs inside, while the tailback can be featured outside as an option runner. The tailback can also run inside, using the fullback as a lead blocker.

The weakness of this attack is that it has a strong side and a weak side, depending on the position of the flanker. Furthermore, this formation does not have a back in position to seal on a linebacker. Many teams have addressed these weaknesses by incorporating other formations into their attacks to complement their base set. For example, Syracuse uses the wishbone in short-yardage situations, and Nebraska uses some one-back and even some I-Bone.

*Coaches who want to learn more about this particular variation of the option attack should visit either Frank Solich at the University of Nebraska or Paul Pasqualoni at Syracuse University and discuss the option game with these two distinguished coaches. Larry Smith of the University of Missouri is another coach whose program combines power and option effectively.

OPTION #38: I-TRAP OPTION

The I-Trap Option is an outstanding misdirection double option play popularized by George DeLeone, the offensive coordinator at Syracuse University. It is set up by establishing the fullback trap, and it calls on the offensive line to use the same blocking scheme it uses in the wing-T trap option (see Option #35). This option is a good way to get the ball pitched to the tailback (Diagram 41).

Assignments:
- The backfield action is similar to that in the Delaware trap option, except for one big difference: the tailback freezes until the quarterback completely turns back to the play side. This freeze by the tailback causes the linebackers to freeze as well, making them more vulnerable to being blocked.

- The fullback dives opposite and fakes the trap.

- The quarterback opens opposite and then turn back into the line of scrimmage and options the defensive end.

- The formation used can be either pro or twins. The play is drawn below with three wide receivers, which was a popular set that George DeLeone frequently employed on this play.

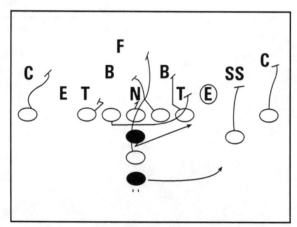

Diagram 41

OPTION #39: FREEZE OPTION

A perfect complement to the trap option is the Freeze Option.* The freeze option was effectively used by Wichita State coach Willie Jefferies and his offensive coordinator, Larry Beckish in the 1970s.

The Freeze Option is blocked exactly like the trap option, but there is a difference in the backfield action. The quarterback opens as he would on the trap option, and the fullback dives to the center, exactly as he would on the trap option. On the Freeze Option, however, the quarterback never turns back, but rather, he continues in the same direction to which he opened. The tailback freezes until the quarterback starts down the line of scrimmage. This action prepares him for a pitch as the quarterback options the defensive end (Diagram 42).

The backfield action in both the trap and freeze should look exactly the same as the play starts. Only after the quarterback comes out of the mesh does the defense know which way the ball is going.

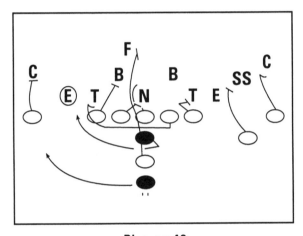

Diagram 42

OPTION #40: FREEZE ARC

A small wrinkle added to the freeze option by Syracuse offensive coordinator George DeLeone was the arcing of the tackle in order to kick out the defender lined up on the wide receiver (Diagram 43). This Freeze Arc scheme is used when there are only six defenders in "the box" and the defense is covering up all the wideouts while playing two deep behind them. The offensive line base blocks the play. This option is similar to a toss sweep to the boundary and is effective against a two-deep defense.

Assignments:
- The onside guard zone blocks the linebacker over him.

- The center and offside line scoop block.

- The onside tackle pulls flat down the line and kicks out the defender on the wideout. Contests will be held on how far tackles can drive the defensive back out of bounds—it's a splatter shot.

- The wide receiver blocks the deep-half defender.

- The backfield action is the same as on the freeze option (see Option #39). The quarterback options the end man on the line of scrimmage.

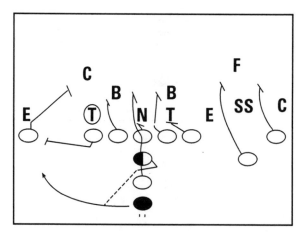

Diagram 43

OPTION #41: POWER I-ISO OPTION

The Power I-Iso Option is an excellent short-yardage offense set up by the isolation play to the tailback. This option is particularly effective against a defense that's overshifting to the power side of the formation (Diagram 44). The offensive line blocks as it would block the isolation play. The I onside guard doubles with the center on the man over the center. The onside tackle reaches the man on him (This move by the tackle represents the only difference between Iso blocking and Iso option blocking). The tight end arcs on the corner.

Assignments:
- The fullback and the tailback both make a great Iso fake. The tailback could even vault into the air as though he had the ball.

- The quarterback reverse pivots and rides the tailback toward the line, faking the Iso; he then comes down the line and options the defensive end. The power back is the pitch back.

The key to this play is a convincing fake of the Iso. The coaching point is that if the corner is on the line, the tight end could block the defensive end while the quarterback options the corner.

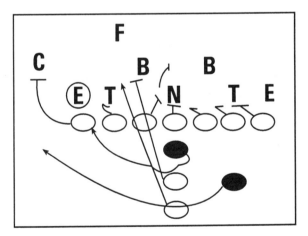

Diagram 44

OPTION #42: I-PRO LEAD OPTION

The I-Pro Lead Option is a simple, yet effective, way to get the ball pitched on the perimeter to the tailback (Diagram 45). The play is run exactly like Option #3—the split-back veer lead option—except the backs are in the I. The fullback is not in as good a lead block position as he is in the split-back set, but he is still effective. The tailback is in better position to get the pitch going downhill, which makes it easier for the play to produce consistent yardage.

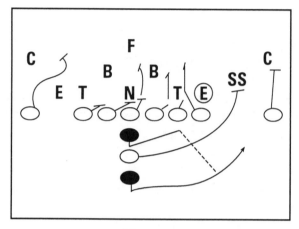

Diagram 45

*The University of Nebraska football team employs a wide variety of options. Coaches who want to learn more about running an option attack from an I formation should consider visiting Lincoln to meet with Frank Solich and his staff to discuss the details of the Cornhuskers' option game.

OPTION #43: I- PRO DOWN OPTION

Another staple of the Nebraska option attack is the I-Pro Down Option from the I formation (Diagram 46).* This option—another double option that can threaten the defense on the perimeter—takes a page from the Delaware Wing-T playbook that is adapted to the I. This play is a very effective option for teams that have a good running quarterback. In it, the offensive line uses the down blocking scheme (see Option #33), and the flanker stalks the corner.

The backfield action is similar to the action in the Delaware down option, except the backs are aligned in the I. The fullback gets on the guard's hip and wraps around for the play-side linebacker (The Delaware down option puts the wing on the linebacker and the fullback on the free safety). The tailback is the pitch man, and the quarterback reverses out and options the defensive end. Coaches should keep in mind that since there is no one on the offense to block the free safety, they must have a down option post pass in the package ready to go.

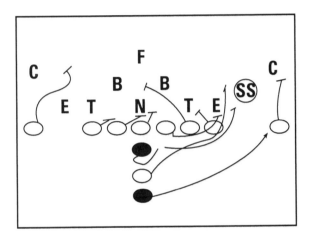

Diagram 46

*Putting the strength into the boundary—through an I-Pro to the Boundary scheme— is another valuable wrinkle in the option attack. The I-Pro to the Boundary attack has two good complementary options with which to work. These options can be packaged effectively as part of the offense's audible game plan.

OPTION #44: I-PRO TRIPLE OPTION

Running the triple option from the I formation and putting the strength to the boundary offers a key advantage: the offensive line can veer block, just as it does in the wishbone (see Option #14). This blocking scheme is especially effective against the overshifted defense.

The assignments are the same as they are in Option #14, except the backs are in the I formation and the flanker stalks the corner. The quarterback reads the triple as he does in any triple option (Diagram 47).

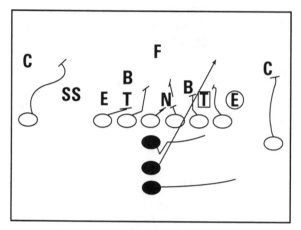

Diagram 47

OPTION #45: I-LEAD OPTION WEAK

The I-Lead Option Weak complements the I-Pro with the strength to the boundary, because it leads the option away from strength or to the field (Diagram 48). This option is the offense's answer if the defense plays two deep or overshifts the front to the boundary. The I-Lead Option Weak is run exactly like the other I-Lead option.

The offensive line seals inside, with the onside tackle and the guard combo blocking the man on the guard to the linebacker (in fact, the tackle and the guard could G block). The rest of the line cuts off. The fullback is the lead blocker; he arc blocks the strong safety. The quarterback drop-steps and options the defensive end. The tailback is the pitch man.

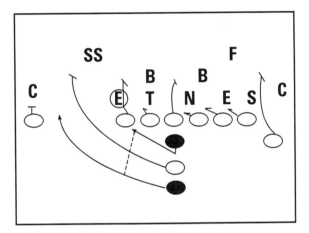

Diagram 48

CHAPTER 8

THE ONE-BACK BONE

One of the recent developments in the evolution of option football has been the employment of the triple option and its companion options from a one-back set. It's been called the Flex Bone by Ken Hatfield and Fisher DeBerry, the Ham Bone by coaches at Georgia Southern (named after quarterback Tracy Ham), the Triple Shoot by some, and the Multi-Bone, which is the name I prefer.*

The idea of a Multiple Bone came to me after hearing Ron Rogerson speak at a camp. Ron was on the Delaware staff and talked about using wingbacks and slots to "get a flank" to run the buck sweep. We decided to use the same idea and run the triple option instead of the buck sweep. The transition was simple; we just moved the halfbacks up to a wing-on-slot position and ran our wishbone plays (Diagram 49). The results were spectacular, and the multi-bone was born. Several other staffs have arrived at the same conclusion, and run their own versions of the one-back wishbone.

*For additional information on the one-back bone, readers should refer to *The Explosive Multi-Bone Attack* (written by Tony DeMeo; published by Harding Press), as well as to four videos on the topic (available from Coaches Choice Books and Videos). Readers might also want to visit with Bob Noblit at Air Force or Paul Johnson at Georgia Southern.

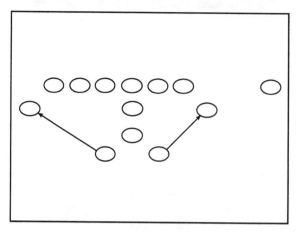

Diagram 49

Advantages of the One-Back Bone

- The obvious benefit of having four receivers on the line of scrimmage is that it enhances the passing game tremendously.

- With an enhanced passing game, the wishbone becomes a legitimate two-minute offense and can help a team come from behind.

- The placement of the halfbacks makes it easier to seal the linebackers, because the halfbacks outflanked them to begin with.

- By virtue of their being on the line of scrimmage, the halfbacks can beat the fullback to the linebacker and effectively seal block for the fullback.

- Because the halfbacks can block for the fullback dive, the offensive line can double-team a tough 3 technique to block the linebacker, instead of using a combo technique (Diagram 50).

- The use of short motion adds speed to the backs because they can now take a running start on their pitch course, rather than having to start from a stationary position.

- Because the passing game becomes a more frequently used part of the offense, coaches find it easier to recruit talented wide receivers.

- The offense becomes more flexible, thus making it easier for coaches to adapt to different personnel from year to year or game to game.

- It is easier to run from a one-back set than to throw from a three-back set.

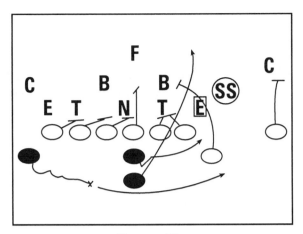

Diagram 50

Disadvantages of the One-Back Bone

- Because the one-back relies on short motion, the coach must make the counter game a big part of his option package.

- The increased use of the passing game accentuates the need for precise time management in practice.

- The quarterback must be a passer as well as a runner so he can take advantage of the four receivers on the line.

- The power game is not as effective from the one-back as it is from the wishbone.

OPTION #46: ONE-BACK LOOP OPTION TO THE TIGHT END

This loop option to the tight end/wingback is especially effective because it takes advantage of a defensive rule of thumb: that it is not sound strategy for a defense to play a hard corner to a wing set, because the wing can threaten the corner very quickly (Diagram 51). This play is executed like the wishbone loop play to the tight end (see Option #12). The advantage in this case is that the tight end pressures the safety, and the wing does the same to the corner. This option works well to the boundary versus a three-deep secondary.

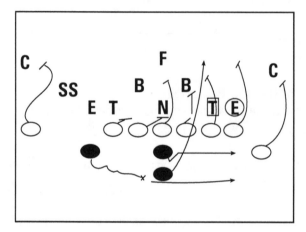

Diagram 51

OPTION #47: ONE-BACK TOAD OPTION

The One-Back Toad Option, a toad option to the tight end/wingback, is a great short-yardage option that can effectively counter a hard corner (Diagram 52). This option is executed exactly like the wishbone toad option (see Option #16), with one coaching point: The wingback must take one step back in order to get an accurate read of the tight end/tackle gap. If that gap is open, the wingback should go through and gore—that's right, gore—the unsuspecting linebacker. His should be a real drill. If the gap is closed, the wingback should go around the tight end's block and seal the linebacker.

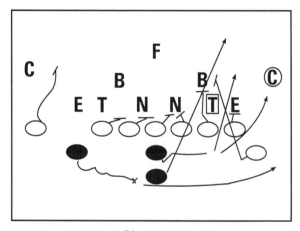

Diagram 52

ГПе Arc Option to the Slot works well against a hard corner. It was run to perfection by I AA gridiron powerhouse Georgia Southern, which used it to win a number of national championships (Diagram 53). With the exception of the slotback and the split end, each player executes as he does in the wishbone arc option (see Option #11).

The split end against a hard corner sets up the slotback's block, faking an outside release and driving up to the free safety. The slot pulls flat down the line of scrimmage and kicks the corner somewhere into the third row. This scheme creates a nice running lane for the pitch back. Against a three-deep look, or in the face of a strong safety, the split end should stalk the corner and the slotback should arc the strong safety.

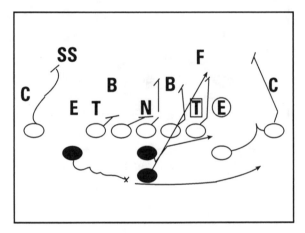

Diagram 53

OPTION #49: SEAL TRIPLE OPTION

The Seal Triple Option is enhanced by the position of the slotback. As mentioned earlier, the slot can block for the fullback (Diagram 50); the slot also outflanks the linebackers by alignment, making the triple option even more effective (Diagram 54).

This play is executed just like the seal option in the wishbone (see Option #17). The line veer blocks and the backfield executes its triple-option assignments. Against a two-deep look, the split end can block the free safety, thus eliminating the free-safety fill.

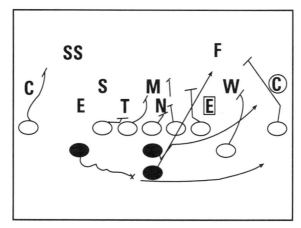

Diagram 54

OPTION #50: LOAD OPTION TO THE SPLIT END

One of the major assets of the one-back bone is that it provides the offense with the ability to run the load option. By his alignment, the slotback outflanks the end man on the line of scrimmage, making it a simple down block to seal the defensive end so that the quarterback can get on the perimeter (Diagram 55).

From the one-back bone, the load option is run as a double option using the Delaware principle of "getting a flank." The offensive line base blocks, but if the onside tackle has the end man on the line of scrimmage on him, he should go up to the linebacker.

In the backfield, the assignments are as follows:

- Onside Slotback—load blocks the end man on the line of scrimmage; he should get a big enough split so he can have an angle on his block.

- Fullback—should start on his triple course and then wrap around the load block and block the linebacker to the safety.

- Offside Slotback—goes in two-step motion and becomes the pitch man.

- Quarterback—flash fakes the fullback and then gets on his outside hip and options the strong safety.

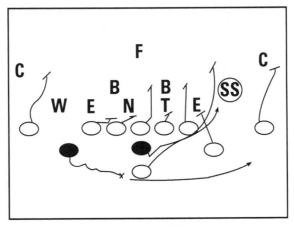

Diagram 55

OPTION #51: LOAD OPTION TO A WING SET

The Load Option to a Wing Set is a guaranteed way to get a flank and thus get the ball on the perimeter. Coaches may prefer running this play to an unbalanced set so the play can be run to the field (Diagram 56).

The play is executed just like the load to the split end side, except it provides an extra blocker with the tight end. Because of the tight end, the wingback will always outflank the defense. The wing and tight end combo block the end man on the line of scrimmage, with the wingback working up to the linebacker. This scheme is a great short-yardage double option, and if the quarterback can scoot, it can produce big gains in every type of situation.

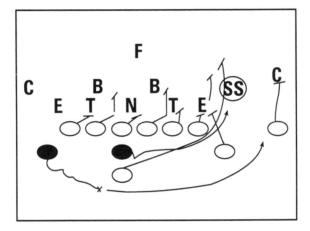

Diagram 56

OPTION #52: CROSS-BLOCK OPTION

The Cross-Block Option from the one-back bone is a great double option taken directly from the Delaware Wing-T playbook, and it is a great way of blocking the free safety and getting the ball on the perimeter (Diagram 57). The play is executed up front exactly like the Delaware Cross-Block Option (see Option #34).

The changes are in assignments are as follows:

- The alignment of the slot provides him with a great angle from which to seal the linebacker.

- The quarterback opens up using his triple step rather than reversing out so he can better see a strong safety blitz.

- The quarterback flash fakes the fullback, who wraps around the guard's block to block the free safety. The quarterback gets on the fullback's hip and executes the option on the strong safety. If the guard cannot log the defensive end, the "duck rule" comes into effect.

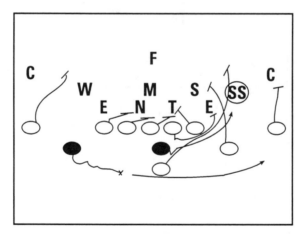

Diagram 57

OPTION #53: DOWN OPTION

The Down Option is another play adapted from the Delaware Wing-T playbook (see Option #33). Again, a few minor differences exist:

- The quarterback and the fullback assignments are the same as in the previous option (Option #52).

- An unbalanced set gives the offense the chance to run this play to the field.

As with Option #52, the big advantage of this particular option is that it enables the fullback to block the alley player (Diagram 58). One important coaching point for the quarterback is that if the guard cannot log the defensive end, then the fullback and the quarterback will have to duck inside the guard's block (once more, invoking the duck rule).

The Down Option is a very effective option designed to take advantage of a quarterback's running ability and to seal the onside linebacker by outflanking him with the wingback. In addition, the fullback has a great opportunity to block the free safety.

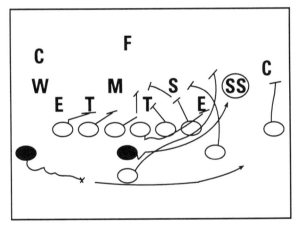

Diagram 58

OPTION #54: QUARTERBACK KEEP TO WING OPTION

A great short-yardage option is the Quarterback Keep to a Wing Option (Diagram 59). Interestingly, this play is really more of a quarterback keep or quarterback Iso than an option. The only time it would become an option is if the defense pinched and forced the ball outside, thus forcing the quarterback to option the corner.

The play is executed exactly like the toad option to the wing (see Option #47). The only difference is that the onside tackle blocks the man on him, which eliminates the quarterback's read and turns the play into a double option. The fullback runs through the guard/tackle gap and Iso blocks the linebacker.

The quarterback flashes the fullback the reads, and the tackles block and duck into the first available daylight. If the defensive tackle widens, the quarterback should follow the fullback through the guard/tackle gap. If the defensive tackle pinches, the quarterback should follow the fullback around the tackle's block and read the tight end's toad block. If the tight end/tackle gap is open, the quarterback should take it himself; but if the defensive end pinches, the quarterback should take it to the corner and option him. This play is an ideal option for a big, strong quarterback who may not be exceptionally fast.

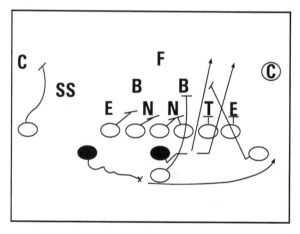

Diagram 59

OPTION #55: QUARTERBACK KEEP FROM THE WISHBONE

Another way to run the quarterback keep is from the wishbone, as in this option play. The quarterback keep can be run exactly the same way, whether it is from the full wishbone or the one-back bone (Diagram 60). This is a very good short-yardage play that provides a nice change of pace from the one-back bone, because you can get the play off on a quick count without motion and catch a defense napping.

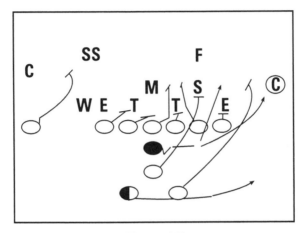

Diagram 60

OPTION #56: ONE-BACK LEAD OPTION

The One-Back Lead Option is an effective way to get the ball pitched to the slotback with a lead blocker. The roots of this play are in either the split-back veer (Option #3) or the lead option from the I (Option #45).

This play is executed exactly like those two particular lead options, the only differences being that the onside slot seals the linebacker and the offside slot goes in motion to be the pitch man (Diagram 61). These two differences are also two big plusses, because the pitch man now can take a running start (rather than having to start from a stationary position, as in the I or split-back veer), and the slot is in perfect position to seal block the play-side linebacker. This play, which was key to Georgia Southern's success, is a simple yet effective double option.

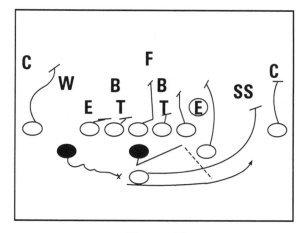

Diagram 61

OPTION #57: COUNTER LEAD OPTION

Another play that was run to perfection by Georgia Southern was the Counter Lead Option to the fullback. The ability to run an option away from motion is essential to the success of the one-back option attack (Diagram 62). The play is blocked just like the split-back veer counter lead option (see Option #7), but is more effective because of the illusion caused by the whirly motion it uses.

The backfield action really sells the counter aspect of this play, because the onside slot goes in whirly motion (i.e., he starts in motion opposite the direction of the play and then turns back and lead blocks play side). The quarterback and the fullback both counter step and then complete their option assignment. This option is an excellent complement to the previous option, and it is also a great way to get a speedy fullback to the perimeter.

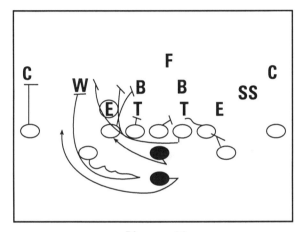

Diagram 62

OPTION #58: TRIPLE AWAY FROM TRIPS

Using multiple formations to run the triple option is one of the most effective ways to keep a defense out of sync. In this Triple Away from Trips set, one of the slotbacks is used as the offside tight end, and both split ends are put to the wide side of the field.*

The option is run exactly like the triple with a loop scheme in other one-back sets (see Option #46), and its effectiveness results from defenses overplaying the trips side (Diagram 63). The main coaching point for the Triple Away from Trips is that the onside slot (disguised as a tight end) arc blocks the corner (as he does from his wing alignment in Option #46). The corner away from trips is usually responsible for the deep third. As a result, he is a "soft corner" and is relatively easy to arc block.

*This option is one of my personal favorites.

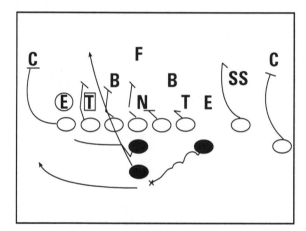

Diagram 63

OPTION #59: TOAD OPTION WITH WHIRLY MOTION

Another effective triple variation is to run it with whirly motion. The Toad Option with Whirly Motion is run exactly like Option #47, except that the wingback uses a whirly motion before executing his seal block. This whirly motion gives a counter effect to the triple option. The toad block buys time for the offside slot to get into pitch phase without motion (Diagram 64). This toad option is a super "counter triple option" that is especially effective in short-yardage situations. The great Chinese philosopher Sun Tsu once said, "War is deception." As such, the Toad Option with Whirly Motion is a very deceptive triple option.

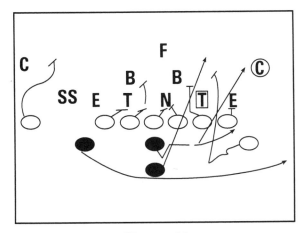

Diagram 64

OPTION #60: TRAP OPTION WITH WHIRLY MOTION

Jacksonville State, when it was the Division II national football champion, made a living running the Trap Option with Whirly Motion (Diagram 65). It is a great double option to the tight end/wing side of the formation. It also has a counter effect because of its whirly motion. The counter game is an essential part of the one-back bone, because defense will try to key in on the short motion.

The offensive line trap-option blocks the play (see Option #38), but the tight end toad blocks the end man on the line. The backfield also executes the normal trap option except that the wingback uses a whirly motion before executing his seal block. If the linebacker has been blocked, the wing should go up to the safety.

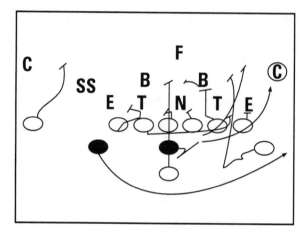

Diagram 65

OPTION #61: TRIPLE OPTION TO TRIPS

Another way to use whirly motion is to make the whirly motion back the pitch man, as in the Triple Option to Trips (Diagram 66). In this play, the line and the backfield execute their normal triple assignments, except that the onside halfback goes into whirly motion and then becomes the pitch man. Again, the whirly motion gives a counter look to the play and also enables the offense to run the triple to or away from trips. This option is a good complement to the option away from trips (see Option #58). At the start of the play, the defense has absolutely no indication of the direction of the play, because the play could be either Option #58 or Option # 61.

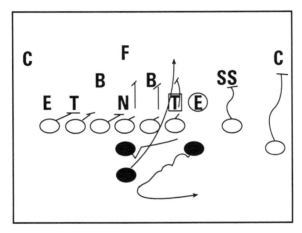

Diagram 66

CHAPTER 9

THE MIDLINE OPTION

Another exciting development in option football has been the coming of age of the midline option.* While it is uncertain who deserves credit for introducing the midline, it is clear that both Mike DeLong, head coach at Springfield College in Massachusetts, and Roy Gregory of Austin Peay, were early users of the midline option. The midline originated from the freeze option. Although it can be run from the I formation, it is probably most effective from a one-back set. Just as the wide veer complemented the triple option (because it moved the play one hole wider), the midline complements the triple option because it hits one hole tighter.

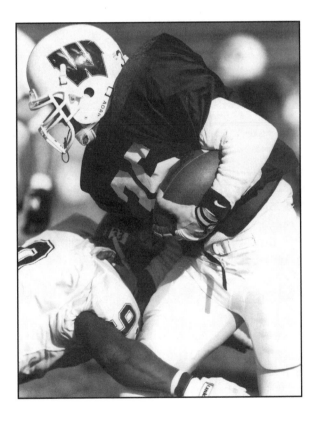

*For more details on the midline option, readers should visit Bob Noblitt of Air Force, Charlie Weatherbee at Navy or Bob Sutton at Army. Coaches are also more than welcome to visit the staff at Washburn or refer to my video on the midline option (available from Coaches Choice Books and Videos).

OPTION #62: MIDLINE TOAD OPTION

The Midline Toad Option is a good triple option to the tight end/wingback side because it provides good blocking angles. It is one of the best options in football today, because it is effective in both short-yardage and normal running situations. While the offensive line's blocking assignments in the Midline Toad Option are relatively simple, they are slightly different from those in the triple option.

Assignments:
- Center—blocks the man onside if he is covered; if he is uncovered, the center seals and then goes up to the back-side linebacker.

- Onside Guard—takes an inside release and blocks the play-side linebacker to the back-side linebacker.

- Onside Tackle—blocks the first linebacker onside or inside.

- Tight End—toad blocks the end man on the line of scrimmage.

- Offside Guard—cuts off and protects the back side of the dive crease.

- Offside Tackle—seals and wheels.

- Backfield—executes its triple-option techniques one hole tighter.

- Fullback—runs the triple option at the butt of the quarterback and blasts through the midline cylinder (the area between the guard/center gaps) as either a ball carrier or a blocker.

- Onside Halfback (wing)—blocks through the guard/tackle gap, blocking the linebacker to the safety.

- Offside Halfback—goes in motion and becomes the pitch man.

- Quarterback—drop steps with his opposite foot to open the midline for the fullback and reads the first man outside the fullback's path; if the ball is pulled, he should option the corner, just as he would in the other toad options (Diagram 67).

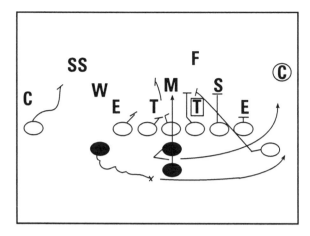

Diagram 67

OPTION #63: MIDLINE TO THE SPLIT END

The Midline to the Split End (or slot side) is also a very effective option play. It is an effective way to run the midline to the wide side of the field. In this option, the offensive line blocks its same midline rules as in the previous play. The backfield also executes the midline as in the previous option, except the onside slotback arc blocks the strong safety. As a result of this adjustment, the quarterback's pitch key is the defensive end (Diagram 68). The main coaching point on this play is that the quarterback, who, because the pitch key is closer, must be prepared to handle quick pressure from the pitch key. The Midline to the Split End is an excellent complement to the tight end/wing midline. It provides the offense with a chance to get the ball pitched to a speedy pitch back. The path of the fullback draws the defense in, and pitching off the defensive end is a very short flank that's conducive to pitching the ball (and putting speed in space).

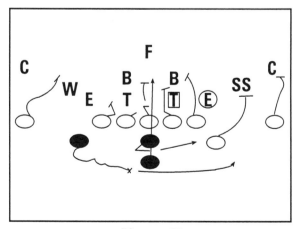

Diagram 68

OPTION #64: LOAD OPTION TO THE SPLIT END

If the pitch key is causing too much pressure on the quarterback, then loading the defensive end on a play like the Load Option to the Split End can solve the problem (Diagram 69). On this play, the slotback loads the defensive end, and the quarterback options the strong safety, thus avoiding the need to make a quick read and pitch of a crash pitch key. The assignments for the Load Option to the Split End are exactly the same as they were in the previous midline triple, except that the onside slot load blocks the defensive end, and the quarterback options the strong safety if the ball isn't given to the fullback.

This play is a low-risk midline triple option to the split end side. Because the load block will delay the pitch possibility, it can be run without motion.

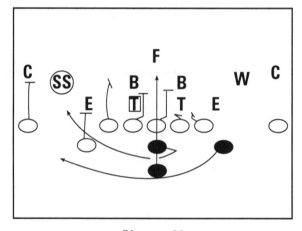

Diagram 69

OPTION #65: MIDLINE LOAD DOUBLE OPTION TO THE SPLIT END SIDE

The Midline Load Double Option to the Split End provides the means to get the ball on the flank by faking the midline dive and having the quarterback take the ball around the load block and option the strong safety (Diagram 70). This is a good double-option complement to the midline triple option. It is especially effective if the inside linebackers are filling hard on the midline.

This option is blocked like the previous option (Option #64), except the onside guard reach blocks the man over him. The quarterback must make a good fake to the fullback, and the fullback must stay in the cylinder to hold the inside linebackers.

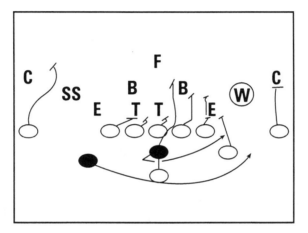

Diagram 70

OPTION #66: LOAD TO THE TIGHT END WITH THE WINGBACK

Another variation of the midline triple option is to Load to the Tight End with the Wingback (Diagram 71). This play is a good short-yardage midline triple option.

On this play, the offensive line blocks normal midline rules, except the onside tackle blocks inside for the inside backer while the tight end releases inside and blocks the outside linebacker. In order to help the wing's load block, the tight end must go through the inside breastplate of the defensive end and thus prevent penetration. The wingback loads the defensive end, and the rest of the backfield executes its normal midline assignment.

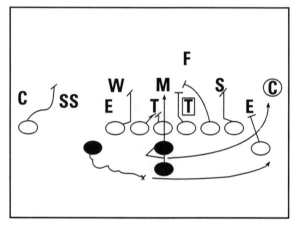

Diagram 71

OPTION #67: TACKLE TOAD TO THE SPLIT END

Blocking the tackle out to the slotback side, as in the Tackle Toad to the Split End, is an excellent way to run the midline (Diagram 72). This option serves as one more way to protect the quarterback from quick pressure from the pitch key. On this play, everyone executes the normal midline triple option, with the following exceptions:

- The onside tackle blocks out on the defensive end, taking him any way he wants to go.

- The onside slotback reads the tackle and seals the play-side linebacker inside or outside the tackle's block.

- The quarterback reads the midline as normal, but if it's a pull read, the quarterback will have to read the tackle's block and either duck inside or go around the tackle's block in order to option the strong safety.

The Tackle Toad to Split End midline triple is both a safe and highly productive option that can be used in a variety of situations. In particular, it can be an effective midline option for a big, strong quarterback who is not blessed with great speed.

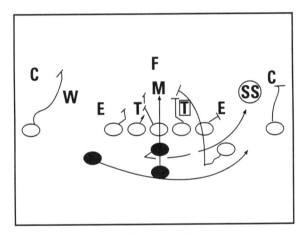

Diagram 72

OPTION #68: LOADED DOUBLE OPTION TO THE WING

The Loaded Double Option to the Wing side is a good addition to the game plan if the linebackers are really filling hard on the dive phase of the midline. This play, which happens to be a good midline to run from an unbalanced formation, is also effective with no motion (Diagram 73).

The assignments on this play are the same as in Option #66, except that the onside guard reach blocks the man on him and, of course, the fullback and the quarterback execute the double option. Both of them should keep in mind the importance of pulling off a really good fake in order to hold the linebackers.

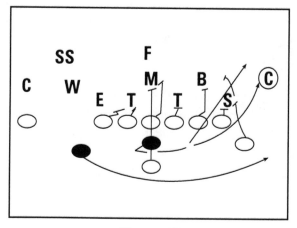

Diagram 73

OPTION #69: MIDLINE PITCH

The Midline Pitch offers another way to get the ball on the perimeter to the halfback. It is especially effective when run from an unbalanced formation, because in that case, a seal blocking scheme can be used (Diagram 74). The Midline Pitch is a good double option to use in order to get the ball pitched off the midline and to take advantage of a gifted halfback. It is also serves to counter linebackers who are filling hard on the dive.

On this play, the offensive line blocks the same as it does in Option #64, and the backfield executes its midline double-option assignments. The only exceptions are that the onside slotback seal blocks linebacker to safety, and the quarterback pitches off the defensive end. When run from an unbalanced set, it calls for the two wide receivers to stalk block the defensive backs over them.

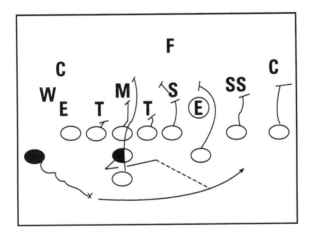

Diagram 74

CHAPTER 10

USING SETS AND MOTION

Unique formations, long motion, and unbalanced formations can all be used by a coach to gain an edge for his team in its option attack. The great advantage of using formation tactics is that they do not require teaching any additional techniques that must be incorporated into the coach's option plays, while they add a great deal of preparation time to his opponents' game plan.

The element of surprise is always another consideration that cannot be underestimated. This section examines three areas on special formations: (1) the use of unbalanced formations, (2) the use of long motion to change the strength of formations, and (3) the running of the option from predominantly passing formations. All three of these concepts are variations that create the perimeter environment conducive to running the option.

Unbalanced Sets
The University of Delaware staff has always done an outstanding job of running the Blue Hens' offensive package from various unbalanced sets. More and more teams, however, have begun adding unbalanced sets to their offensive arsenal. The next few options in this chapter provide examples of how a coach can adapt an unbalanced set to his team's attack. While previous chapters have already touched on a few unbalanced options (e.g., Option #15, Option #53, and Option #68) that readers can go back and review, this chapter will look at even more examples of how to exploit unbalanced formations.

OPTION #70: I TWINS OVER TRIPLE OPTION

Using twins over, as in I Twins over Triple Option, gives an offense the chance to not only use veer blocking, but to also handle a tough nose guard. This triple option with veer blocking is run like the others. The tight end inside releases and blocks linebacker to safety, and the two wideouts stalk block the defenders over them (Diagram 75). This option is similar to the bone over option (see Option #15). Another advantage of this scheme is that by veer blocking, the offense will entice the defense to mirror the scheme and close down, thus giving the quarterback a good pitch possibility. This option also facilitates the pitch to the tailback.

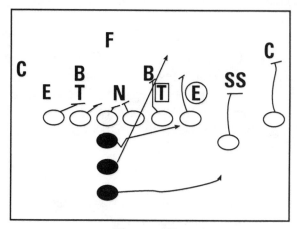

Diagram 75

OPTION #71: ONE-BACK UNBALANCED

Taking both wide receivers and putting them to the same side of the formation gives an offense the ability to block the free-safety alley player (Diagram 76). Other than the inside split end blocking the free safety, the One-Back Unbalanced is executed like Option #49. It is a simple yet very effective adjustment that will defeat the dreaded free-safety fill. Coaches and players should never limit themselves to the idea that throwing the post route will be enough to discourage the free-safety fill. Although the post route is one answer to exploiting this defensive ploy, it is the unbalanced set that keeps the option game productive.

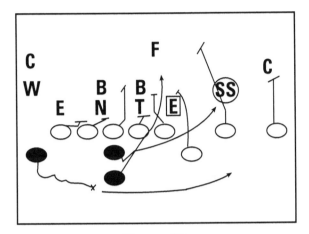

Diagram 76

OPTION #72: BONE OVER PITCH PLAY

Another variation of the option is to use an unbalanced formation and pitch the ball off the handoff key. The offensive line loop blocks, and the tight end toad blocks the end man on the line (the pitch key). The running backs run their triple course and the quarterback flash fakes the fullback and options the handoff key.

This play should work as an excellent toss sweep and provide the offense with yet another way of featuring their halfback and putting speed in space (Diagram 77). Occasionally, defenses will try to eliminate the pitch phase of the triple option, making it difficult to get the halfback the ball. The Bone Over Pitch Play can counter that defensive strategy.

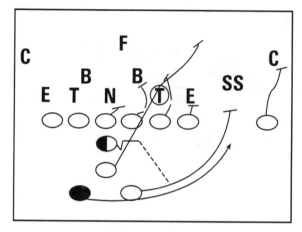

Diagram 77

OPTION #73: ONE-BACK PITCH PLAY

The same concept displayed in Option #72 is possible from a one-back unbalanced set. The One-Back Pitch Play is blocked the same way as in Option #72, except the two wideouts stalk the secondary. The advantages of using this set are (1) the pitch back has a running start and (2) the twin wide receiver is in position to run a dump route. This option facilitates getting the ball to the halfback on a pitch play, especially if the defense is denying the pitch (Diagram 78).

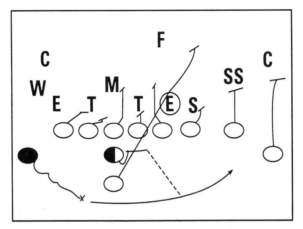

Diagram 78

OPTIONS FROM PASSING SETS

Effective counters to the blitz or man-to-man are plays that enable the offense to either check to an option from an "obvious" pass set and those that work well as part of a two-minute or long-yardage package. The run-and-shoot architects, for example, have always used some aspects of the option game. Mouse Davis had success with the lead option to the fullback in various situations and especially on the goal line. The University of Nebraska added the option from its shotgun offense and was very productive. At James Madison, we used the option from a no-back set, because many defensive coordinators like to play man-to-man versus no-backs, or else they like to blitz when they see the backfield empty.

The whole idea of running the option from a one-back set was to be able to spread a defense and threaten it vertically with four receivers on the line of scrimmage. Running the option from passing sets affords the offense the advantage of running against a pass defense.

OPTION #74: RUN-AND-SHOOT OPTION

The Pitch Option to Trips is a favorite play of the Run-and-Shoot proponents. In it, the offensive line uses its lead option rules (see Option #48). However, the backfield play is a little different in that the onside slotback seals the linebacker, and the wide receivers stalk block. The fullback is the pitch man, and the quarterback options the end man on the line (Diagram 79). The run-and-shoot works very well against man-to-man defenses, which are common against run-and-shoot teams.

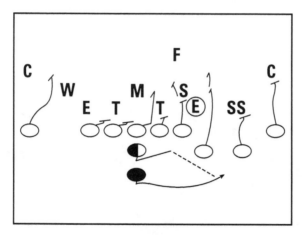

Diagram 79

OPTION #75: DOUBLE PRO OPTION

One of the plays that Kordell Stewart ran to perfection at the University of Colorado was the zone option from a double pro formation, the Double Pro Option (Diagram 80).* This option works best against a defensive end with an inside shade on the tight end. It is also very effective from an I-Pro formation and is a favorite of Larry Smith at the University of Missouri (Diagram 80A). In the Double Pro Option, the line zone blocks the front, with the key block being the combo block by the onside tackle and the tight end. The tackle must overtake the tight end's block, which will allow the tight end to work up to the linebacker. A key to this block is for the tackle to drop step before reaching the defensive end.

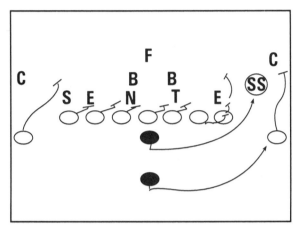

Diagram 80

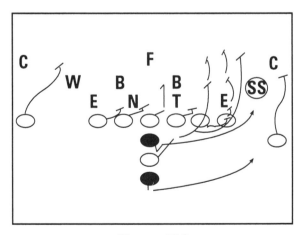

Diagram 80A

*Coaches who are interested in running this scheme might consider taking a trip to Lincoln to visit with Frank Solich and his staff at the University of Nebraska.

OPTION #76: SHOTGUN ARC OPTION

The Shotgun Arc Option is another play that is executed brilliantly by the Cornhuskers of Nebraska. This option works very well against nickel-and-dime defenses. It also underscores one of the premises of option football: make pass defenders play the run.

The Shotgun Arc Option calls for the line to block lead option rules, with the onside slot arc blocking either the outside linebacker or the nickel back. The setback bubbles back to become the pitch back, and the quarterback receives the snap from the center and options the end man on the line (Diagram 81). Because of his alignment, the quarterback must approach the pitch key on a downhill course.

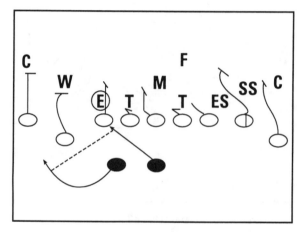

Diagram 81

OPTION #77: SHOTGUN LOAD OPTION

A variation of the previous option (#76) is the Shotgun Load Option. It is executed exactly as the previous option, except the slot load blocks the defensive end, and the quarterback now options the outside linebacker or the nickel back (Diagram 82).

The Shotgun Load Option is good counter to the blitz and also comes in handy if the outside linebacker is too tough to arc block. If the outside linebacker or the nickel back walks up on the line of scrimmage (thus making it difficult for him to be arc blocked), this play could be an automatic check from the arc option play.

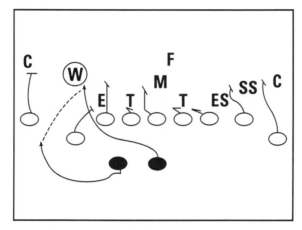

Diagram 82

OPTION #78: NO-BACK OPTION

Many defenses make an automatic man call versus a no-backer. They also are always on guard for the quarterback draw. These defensive adjustments help make the option a devastating tool. The No-Back Option is one such tool. It is executed like the run-and-shoot option (see Option #74) with one exception: Instead of the run-and-shoot fullback being the pitch man, the back-side slotback goes in motion to become the pitch man (Diagram 83). In addition to destroying man coverage, this play gives the offense the chance to pitch the ball to a speedy wide receiver or halfback with a running start.

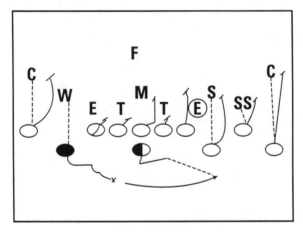

Diagram 83

OPTION #79: NO-BACK WHIRLY OPTION

A great complement to the previous option (#78) is the No-Back Whirly Option. On this play, the motion man uses a whirly motion and then runs the option to the back side (Diagram 84). This option will negate the effectiveness of a defender who is trying to run with motion. Options #78 and #79 can both be run to either side, providing four good options from a no-back set. The combination of these options destroys any motion key the defense has, because regardless of the direction of the motion, the play could go either way.

EXTENDED MOTION

Long or extended motion offers a few very sound advantages for option football, including:

- It changes the strength of the formation, forcing a secondary adjustment that provides a soft flank.

- It exposes man-to-man defenses.

- It creates a numbers advantage against a three-deep or nonadjusting secondary.

- When run from a backfield set, it adds an additional receiver on the line of scrimmage and changes the strength of the formation.

- It frees up the receiver from bump or star coverages.

Long motion can be added to any option offense in order to provide a little spice to a team's perimeter game. Long motion also can be combined with unbalanced or other exotic sets in an effort to really push defenses over the edge and defensive coordinators into the insurance business.

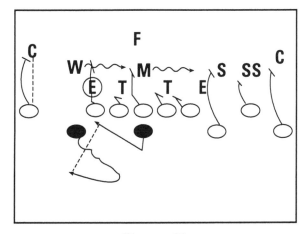

Diagram 84

OPTION #80: DOUBLE PRO ZONE OPTION

By adding extended motion to the Double Pro Zone Option, the free safety can be blocked (Diagram 85). This option play is executed like Option #75. The only teaching to do is to instruct the motion man to block the free safety, which is also another way of handling the dreaded alley player. This option also lends itself to the skills of a good rushing quarterback.

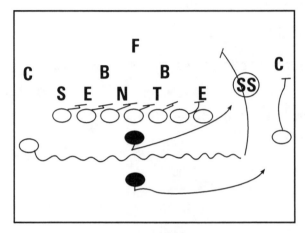

Diagram 85

OPTION #81: DOUBLE PRO LEAD OPTION

Another simple adjustment that the offense can make with long motion is to run a lead option from a one-back set, as in the Double Pro Lead Option. In this option, the offensive line blocks just as it would in the split-back veer option (see Option #3). The flanker cracks the strong safety, and the motion man kicks out the corner, leaving a nice running lane for the pitch man. The quarterback drop-steps and options the end man on the line, and the fullback is the pitch man (Diagram 86).

One big advantage to running the Double Pro Lead Option is that blocking the tight end down forces the defensive end close, with the tight end thus giving the quarterback the probability of a pitch to the tailback. In addition, by using motion, the offense is likely to get a soft flank, as well as relatively easy blocks for the wideouts.

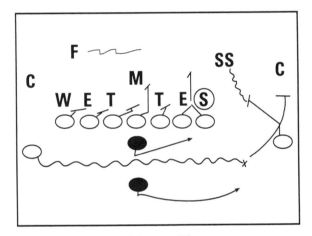

Diagram 86

OPTION #82: RUN-AND-SHOOT OPTION WEAK

If a defense is playing man-to-man against the run-and-shoot, the lead option away from motion provides the offense with a nice, short flank and a good opportunity to get the ball pitched. The Run-and-Shoot Option Weak is executed just like the normal run-and-shoot option (see Option #74), but away from long motion (Diagram 85). This is a great red-zone option to use against a defense that has a blitz-man tendency there. Larry Zierlein, when he was coordinating Mouse Davis's offense with the New York Knights in the WFL, made great use of this play on the goal line.

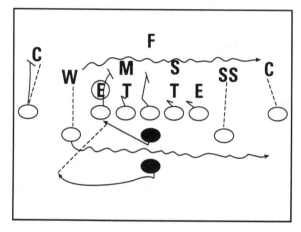

Diagram 87

OPTION #83: RUN-N- SHOOT OPTION STRONG

Of course, the complement to the option away from motion is the option to motion. If the defense is in a zone defense and does not adjust to the extended motion, then the offense gains a numbers advantage to the motion side (Diagram 88). The assignments in the Run-and-Shoot Option Strong are the same as those in the run-and-shoot option to trips (see Option #74), except this scheme calls for the onside split end to crack the strong safety and the motion man to kick out the corner in order to provide a running lane for the pitch man. The quarterback should force the pitch key to play him by attacking the inside shoulder of the pitch key and using a "pitch unless..." thought process.

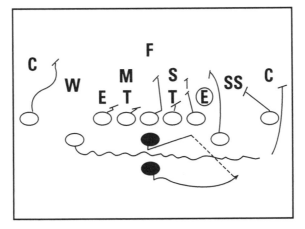

Diagram 88

OPTION #84: I FORMATION MOTION

Motioning from twins to pro makes the secondary adjust and provide a soft flank. This motion also causes the free safety to become a support defender and the strong safety to play the deep third (i.e., the offensive scheme makes run defenders play pass and pass defenders play run). Any I option can benefit from this perimeter tactic, and the Syracuse Trap Option (Diagram 89) is an excellent example. This option is executed just like Option #38, except that by adding motion, it becomes more dynamic and gives the offense a good chance to eliminate the dreaded alley player because the tight end is in position to block the free safety.

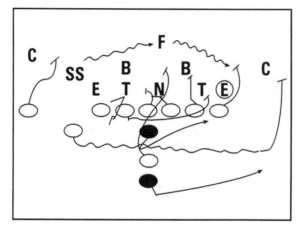

Diagram 89

OPTION #85: MOTION TO I UNBALANCED

Another play used by George DeLeone, the offensive coordinator at Syracuse University, is one in which the split end steps off the line of scrimmage and the flanker sets up on the line. The split end then goes in motion, creating a twins over formation. Any option can be run from this alignment, but the I lead option is especially enhanced, because the motion man can set up the fullback's block on the strong safety and then block the free safety, who is the alley player (Diagram 90). The rest of the play is run like the regular I lead option (see Option #40). The use of motion on this play solves two problems for the offense: (1) it softens the strong safety's run support and (2) it provides another way of blocking the free-safety fill.

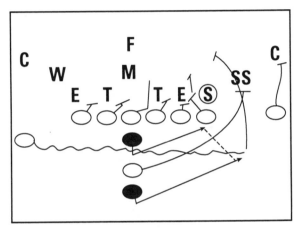

Diagram 90

OPTION #86: ONE-BACK BONE WITH NO-PITCH OPTION

An excellent way to keep defenses off balance is to put a slot in motion in order to get into trips and then run the dive/keep phase of the triple option. This long-yardage play is called the One-Back Bone with No-Pitch Option (Diagram 91). It can be a backbreaker for a defense that sees long motion and then gets into a pass defense or a pass-rush attitude up front.

The no-pitch option is executed exactly like the normal seal triple option (Option #49), but instead of pitching off the strong safety, the man in motion blocks him. The quarterback reads the handoff key normally, but if it's a pull read, he keeps the football. In essence, this play is a double (give/keep) option. The extended motion on the play gives the illusion of a pass formation and keeps the defense off balance. It can also thwart a defense that's keying on the lead option to the fullback (Option #83) by putting its defensive end upfield when it sees long motion.

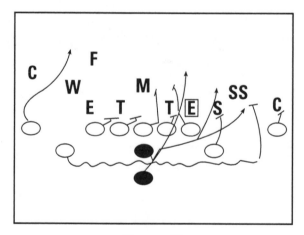

Diagram 91

OPTION #87: NO-PITCH MIDLINE

The same concept underpinning Option #86 can be used for the midline option. In the No-Pitch Midline, the quarterback either gives or keeps, but the motion man blocks the pitch key, thus eliminating the pitch phase of the midline triple option (Diagram 92). The rest of the play is run like the standard midline triple option (Option #67).

These no-pitch options (Options #86 and #87) are good key breakers and also excellent long-yardage options when the defense is thinking pass rush and is taking the bait of the long motion. In addition, these options require very little teaching, because the basic plays involved are the same.

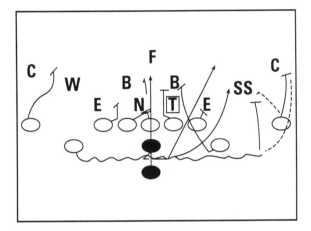

Diagram 92

OPTION #88: WISHBONE FULLBACK MOTION I

Another good addition to the wishbone option package is the Wishbone Fullback Motion I, which puts the fullback in motion to the split end before running the lead double option (Option #56). On this play, the offensive line blocks just as it does on the lead option, except the onside halfback seals the onside linebacker from the backfield using the same technique as in the seal option from the wishbone (Option #17). The split end cracks the strong safety and the fullback stays on a flat path and kicks out the corner, giving the pitch man a good running lane. The quarterback runs the play like the lead option, pitching off the defensive end and getting the ball on the perimeter (Diagram 93). This option offers an excellent opportunity to get the ball pitched to a gifted halfback while again softening the flank (Diagram 93A).

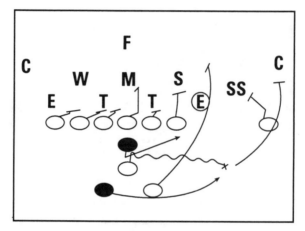

Diagram 93

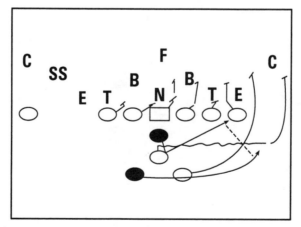

Diagram 93A

OPTION #89: WISHBONE FULLBACK MOTION II

The obvious complement to the previous option is the lead arc option away from the fullback motion to the tight end side (see Diagram 94). This option is run exactly like the split-back veer lead option (see Option #3) and is a simple, effective way to get the ball pitched on the perimeter. The motion forces secondary adjustment, thus it takes the free safety out of a position to fill. Blocking the tight end down causes the defensive end to close, which enhances the quarterback's ability to pitch the ball (The pitch on the perimeter makes the most of the principles of "points" and "speed in space"). Option #88 lends itself more to an eight-man front, while Option #89 works best against a seven-man front. In order to maximize his use of personnel, the coach may choose to slip a wide receiver into the fullback position when running these long-motion options.

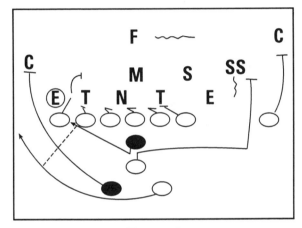

Diagram 94

OPTION #90: WISHBONE HALFBACK MOTION

The Wishbone Halfback Motion is yet another effective short-yardage or goal-line scheme that's run out of the wishbone. The object is to send the onside halfback in motion to widen the corner. The triple option is then run with veer blocking, with the tight end releasing inside and blocking the linebacker to the safety (Diagram 95). This option is similar to Option #14, except that the halfback arc blocks the corner after going in motion rather than doing so from the backfield. This option, long a staple of the Syracuse offense, is effective against an eight-man front or away from the strong safety.

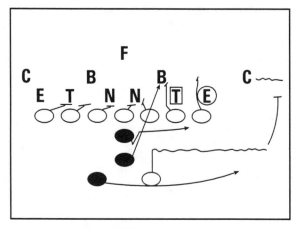

Diagram 95

OPTION #91: WISHBONE CROSS HALF MOTION

The Wishbone Cross Half Motion complements Option #90 by putting the opposite halfback in motion, thus creating a heavy set. Although this is a great formation from which to either sprint out or run flood patterns, it is also an effective way to run a safe no-pitch option from the wishbone alignment.

One of the best options to use in this scheme is the toad option (see Option #16), except without a pitch back. In other words, this option is another give or keep play, with the motion halfback blocking the pitch key, instead of the quarterback optioning him (Diagram 96). The principle used in this option is the same one that's used in Option #86.

This great short-yardage option is enhanced by the use of motion, which stretches the defense. The motion also opens up a world of potential flood and sprint-out passes. The defense must view this formation as a passing set.

Putting one of the backs in motion from the wishbone opens up many possibilities and enhances the passing game by putting three receivers on the line of scrimmage. On the goal line there are many cluster routes or mismatches that the offense can create in its passing attack by using this Wishbone Cross Half Motion.

*No-pitch options are low-risk options that work well when an offense is trying to run out the clock. Paul Pasqualoni of Syracuse University has successfully used many of these multi-bone wrinkles. Readers who would like more information on this topic may want to refer to the book *The Explosive Multi-Bone Attack* (by Tony DeMeo; published by Harding Press).

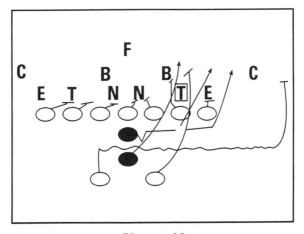

Diagram 96

CHAPTER 11

GADGET OPTIONS

Gadgets, rooskies, and flea-flickers can be a "fun" part of a football game. The players love them and so do the fans—when they work. A number of gadget plays are especially conducive to option football. When used and executed properly, these gadget options keep a defense on its heels and help drain some of its aggressiveness. This section will explore three areas of gadget options: (1) reverse options, (2) pass/run options, and (3) upside-down options.

Reverse Options
Reverse options are good misdirection options that are very effective in getting the ball to the wide receiver. If a team is blessed with a talented wide receiver, the more times he gets his hands on the ball, the more productive that offense will be. Keep in mind that one of the basic premises of this book is the idea of getting speed in space.

Reverse options are more effective than simple reverses, because if the offense runs a simple reverse and the back-side defensive end plays upfield, the runner will most likely be thrown for a big loss. However, if the offense runs a reverse option and the defensive end defends the reverse, the quarterback can duck inside for positive yardage.

OPTION #92: SPLIT-BACK REVERSE OPTION

The Split-Back Reverse Option was developed by Cincinnati's Homer Rice, when he was wrecking defenses with his split-back veer attack. The play calls for the offensive line to block just as it does on the counter dive option (see Option #4). The only coaching point is that the onside tackle can use a reverse crab technique on this play. The rest of the assignments are as follows:

- The onside split end stalks the deep third defender.

- The backfield executes a double-dive fake. Both running backs must make good dive fakes and dent the line of scrimmage.

- The quarterback flash fakes the counter dive and then comes down the line of scrimmage to option the end man on the line. The key coaching point for the quarterback is to expect a crash defensive end and be prepared to pitch it quickly.

- The slot receiver comes around and runs through the heels of the slot's original alignment and is the pitch man (Diagram 97).

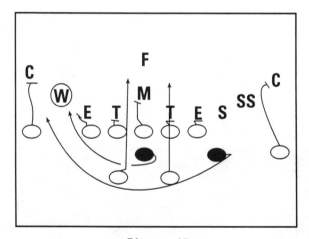

Diagram 97

OPTION #93: ISO REVERSE OPTION

A great short-yardage or goal-line reverse option with big-play potential is the Iso Reverse Option. This reverse option comes off the fake of the isolation play to the tailback and is an effective key breaker. The play is executed exactly like the Iso option described earlier (see Option #45), but with a couple of key variations:

- A wide receiver in the slot position enables the offense to threaten the defense with the prospect of getting the ball to its speediest runner.

- The tight end toad blocks the end man on the line of scrimmage. This block makes the fake of the Iso more convincing and also protects the quarterback from quick pressure by the defensive end, a normal occurrence in short-yardage situations.

As this option plays out, the quarterback fakes the Iso and really sinks the fake (Because of the toad block, he will have more time to sell the fake). The quarterback accelerates out of his fake and reads the tight end's block. If the tight end has the defensive end hooked, the quarterback options the corner. If the defensive end plays wide, then the quarterback must duck inside and get the first down or score a touchdown. The slot comes around through the heels of the fullback's original alignment and is the pitch man (Diagram 98).

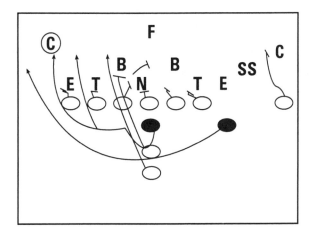

Diagram 98

Pass/Run Options

A pass/run option is one that begins initially as a pass play and then develops into an option play if the pass phase of the play is defended. The concept of the play is to attack the force defender in the secondary; if he comes upfield to play option, the zone he vacates is open for a pass play. If, however, the force defender reads pass and drops off into coverage, the quarterback simply continues down the line of scrimmage to execute the option off that force defender.

Options #94–#97 represent a sampling of these pass/run options, or dump passes. Keep in mind that all of these "dump options" are adaptable to any offense. (Note: Legendary high school coach Frank Glazier, founder of the Frank Glazier Clinics, was the master of the dump pass and had it down to a science.)

OPTION #94: I TWINS OVER DUMP PASS

The I Twins Over Dump Pass is a wonderful complement to the triple option to I twins over, because anytime the twin receiver is having difficulty blocking the strong safety, the dump pass will solve that problem. The play is blocked exactly like the triple option, except the onside tackle blocks base and the tight end toad blocks the end man on the line. The line must sell the run by aggressively run blocking.

The backfield executes the triple option, but in this case the fullback is responsible for the onside linebacker. The tailback takes his pitch course. The quarterback fakes the fullback and then comes down the line of scrimmage, stuttering his feet to slow down so he can read the strong safety. He throws the ball to the twin receiver unless the strong safety covers him. If the strong safety covers the dump pass, the quarterback executes the option off the strong safety (Diagram 99). The quarterback's rule is simple: Read the strong safety. If he comes, then throw the football. If he drops, then run it.

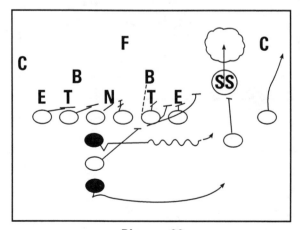

Diagram 99

OPTION #95: TRIPS HOT OPTION

The Trips Hot Option is a pass off the fullback option that attacks a linebacker who fills on run or is too tight to defend the "hot" throw to the onside slot. This play is an excellent companion to Option #83 and is executed exactly the same way, except for the assignments for the onside slot and the quarterback:

- Instead of sealing the play-side linebacker, the onside slot widens his alignment, gets width on his release, and looks for the ball. If the linebacker covers him and he doesn't get the hot pass, he simply blocks the linebacker.

- The quarterback takes his drop step and looks at the play-side linebacker. If the linebacker does anything but cover the hot slot, the quarterback throws the ball to the slot on his first drop step. If the linebacker gets width and is in the throwing lane, the quarterback comes down the line and options the defensive end (Diagram 100).

The Trips Hot Option includes two key coaching points. First, the fullback must drop step in order to get the proper relationship. Second, the onside must release with width in order to stretch the linebacker.

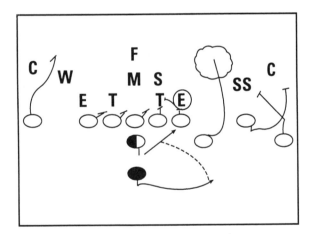

Diagram 100

OPTION #96: SLANT OPTION

The Slant Option can be run a number of ways. However, it is particularly effective as a simple, productive way to attack the strong safety by using long motion and complementing the run-and-shoot fullback option (see Option #83). This play is blocked the same as the pure run, with the exception of the onside slot. In order to give the quarterback more time to make his decision, the onside slot must load the end man on the line. The quarterback comes down the line of scrimmage and finds the strong safety. The quarterback is going to throw the slant route every time, unless the strong safety drops to cover it. If the strong safety drops, the quarterback continues down the line and options the strong safety with the fullback as his pitch man (Diagram 101).

The Slant Option provides yet another way of exploiting an aggressive strong safety who is difficult to block. One principle of offense is to constantly present the defense with conflicts to its keys. It is sequence football: if the defense stops one play, it is only succeeding in opening up another play for the offense.

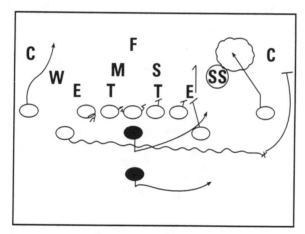

Diagram 101

OPTION #97: COUNTER TRAP SLANT OPTION

A variation of the slant option is the Counter Trap Slant Option. This play also attacks the strong safety, but it adds counter action in the backfield that freezes the linebackers and diverts them from their pass drops. Another addition, a pulling guard, tends to deceive a defense that's reading the offensive line for pass cues. Using the run-blocking scheme makes the run and the pass look identical. The Counter Trap Slant Option comes in handy for teams that don't have a particularly good runner at quarterback, because it's a pass or pitch option, not a keep or pitch option.

This play is executed like Option #7, with a few variations:

- The pulling guard blocks the end man on the line instead of turning up on the linebacker, as he does in the option. This block protects the quarterback and buys him time to read the strong safety.

- The widest receiver runs a slant route.

- The inside receiver arcs on the corner.

- The quarterback executes the counter trap option, but comes down the line and reads the strong safety. He throws the slant unless the strong safety is in the throwing lane. If the strong safety is in the lane, the quarterback pitches to the offside halfback (Diagram 102).

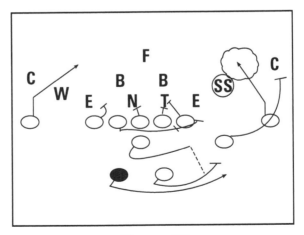

Diagram 102

Upside-Down Options

Upside-down options are variations of the old shovel pass. Although this type of play is referred to here as an option, it is also a pass play, because the quarterback pitches the ball forward, thus making it a forward pass. However, it still qualifies as an option, too, because the quarterback has a pitch/keep decision to make. This is a safe pass or option play, because a fumbled pitch counts as merely an incomplete pass. The upside-down play is a good play to turn to when an offense is protecting a lead and is faced with a passing situation.

OPTION #98: TRIPS SHOVEL

The Trips Shovel, which is highlighted by a high-percentage shovel pass to the offside tight end, helps negate the impact of a tough defensive end who is difficult for the fullback to block on the sprint-out pass (Diagram 103). The Trips Shovel is blocked as though it were the lead option (Option #3) and gets a good double-team at the point of attack. The fullback attacks the defensive end, but takes an inside-out angle; he then passes the defensive end and seals on the onside linebacker.

The quarterback gets depth on his sprint/pass course and reads the defensive end. He then pitches to the back-side tight end unless the defensive end comes down, in which case, he should keep the ball on a quarterback sweep.

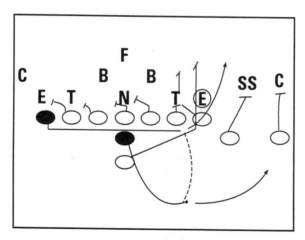

Diagram 103

OPTION #99: NO-BACK SHOVEL

The No-Back Shovel can be an effective shovel against man coverage. This play is executed exactly as the previous shovel-pass play, except that the fullback goes in motion away from the play. This motion will cause the linebackers to adjust and open up the shovel pass (Diagram 104). If no one covers the fullback, the quarterback can use the "uncovered rule and pick up and throw him the ball.

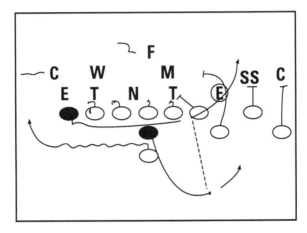

Diagram 104

CHAPTER 12

KICKING-GAME OPTIONS

Option plays can be used very effectively in kicking situations to fake out the defense. This section offers two simple options for the kicking game: one from a punt formation and one from either a PAT or a field goal formation. Of course, many types of options can be used with the kicking game. Coaches are limited in their arsenal of options only by the scope of their imagination.

OPTION #100: FAKE PUNT OPTION

The Fake Punt Option can be executed from any of the standard punt formations, but for simplicity's sake, the spread punt set will serve as the backdrop for this option. Incidentally, this option is particularly effective against a defense that likes to rush inside.

The offensive line executes the lead option (Option #3), as described throughout this book. The onside slot load blocks the first man outside the tackle's block, as long as this man is *not* the end man on the line of scrimmage. Most likely, the punt-return team will be in a gap rush; therefore, these gap blocks by the line and the slot should be relatively easy to make.

The center snaps the ball to the personal protector, who options the first man outside the slot's block. The punter becomes the pitch man (Diagram 105). This is a simple fake punt that capitalizes on option principles.

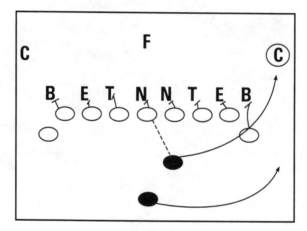

Diagram 105

OPTION #101: FAKE FIELD GOAL OPTION

The Fake Field Goal Option is essentially the same play as the fake punt option, except that it is run from a field goal set. The linemen and the wingback gap block everything inside to create a seal for the option. The ball is snapped to the holder, who straightens up and options the first man outside the wingback's block. The kicker then becomes the pitch man (Diagram 106).

If the defense uses an overload rush, this option can be checked away from the overload. This play will result in a productive fake if the offense has less than four yards to go for either a first down or a touchdown. It can also be used effectively on a two-point conversion attempt.

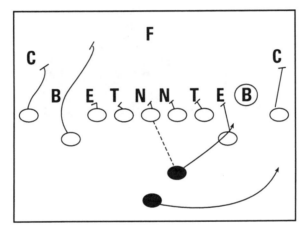

Diagram 106

Tony DeMeo is the head football coach at Washburn University in Topeka, Kansas. When he accepted his current position in December of 1993, DeMeo brought a new offense, a new philosophy, and a new attitude to the Ichabod gridiron efforts. Those attributes have restored respectability to the Washburn program. DeMeo has also served as head football coach at Mercyhurst College in Erie, Pennsylvania (1981-87), and Iona College in New Rochelle, New York (1975-78).

In addition to his head coaching experience, DeMeo has served as an offensive coordinator at James Madison University (1990), Murray State University (1992), and Temple University (1988). He has been an assistant coach on the football staffs of the University of Delaware (1989), University of Massachusetts (1991), University of Pennsylvania (1979-80), and Pace University (1973-74).

An accomplished speaker and a gifted writer, DeMeo has authored three books, has produced four instructional videos, and has been the featured presenter at more than 600 events including football clinics, sports banquets, business seminars, and fund-raisers. DeMeo is a native of the Bronx, New York, and a graduate of Iona college (1971). He currently lives in Topeka, Kansas, with his wife, Joanne, and their four daughters, Sara, Annie, Mary Kate, and Michelle.

ADDITIONAL FOOTBALL RESOURCES FROM

VIDEOS FEATURING TONY DEMEO

COACHING THE TRIPLE OPTION
1998 • Running Time: 58 min.
ISBN 1-57167-219-2 • $40.00

COACHING THE MIDLINE AND THE DOUBLE OPTION
1998 • Running Time: 66 min.
ISBN 1-57167-220-6 • $40.00

THE 5-STEP DROP AND THE TRIPLE SCREEN
1998 • Running Time: 56 min.
ISBN 1-57167-221-4 • $40.00

SPRINT OUT PASSING GAME AND THE 3-STEP BOOT
1998 • Running Time: 52 min.
ISBN 1-57167-222-2 • $40.00

TO PLACE YOUR ORDER OR FOR A FREE CATALOG:
U.S. customers call
TOLL FREE: (800)327-5557
or visit our website at
www.coacheschoice-pub.com
or FAX: (217) 359-5975
or write
COACHES CHOICE™
P.O. Box 647, Champaign, IL 61824-0647